N o r t h

S e a

tic

n

Marston Moor

Adwalton Moor

Naseby

Edgehill

Chalgrove

Newbury 1 & 2

English   Channel

DEATH,
DESTRUCTION
AND A PACKET OF PEANUTS

DEATH,
DESTRUCTION
AND A PACKET OF PEANUTS

BEING A ROLLICKING PUB CRAWL
THROUGH FOUR YEARS OF THE

ENGLISH
 Civil War

BY
CHRIS PASCOE
SOMETIME

Drinker at the Battlefields of EDGEHILL, ADWALTON MOOR,
MARSTON MOOR, NASEBY *&c.*

PORTICO

First published in the United Kingdom in 2009 by
Portico Books
10 Southcombe Street
London
W14 0RA

An imprint of Anova Books Company Ltd

ISBN 9781906032623

A CIP catalogue record for this book is available from the British Library.

10 9 8 7 6 5 4 3 2 1

Typeset by SX Composing DTP, Rayleigh, Essex
Printed and bound by WS Bookwell, Finland

This book can be ordered direct from the publisher.
Contact the marketing department, but try your bookshop first.

www.anovabooks.com

With thanks to Lorraine, Maya, Pete Ilic, Eve White, Tom Bromley and Malcolm Croft

Contents

The Mission

In which the Author, against his will, is forced to get drunk and write a book

My reasons for writing this book were manifold. Money was a good one. As was an almost obsessive interest in the English Civil War, stretching back to childhood.

I still remember my first Civil War re-enactment. I sat upon a damp hillside in Hemel Hempstead, an over-excited eight-year-old waiting expectantly for Roundheads and Cavaliers to start pounding and piking one another to death in the field below, that being the sort of thing they seemed to enjoy.

My parents had bought me a small flag, so I could cheer on my side in the forthcoming bloodbath. I'd read quite a bit about the war. I knew all the commanders' names, the weapons used and the battles fought. But I'd never seen a flag like this one. It just didn't seem in keeping with seventeenth-century England. Too fancy, too glitzy, too star-splattered.

So I waved my Confederate flag and watched in utter confusion as the Army of North Virginia launched a deafening cannonade across Gettysburg Field into the massed Yankees before them. The motley grey-clad rebels followed the cannon shot in, marching steadily towards the lines of blue, sounding blood-curdling rebel yells and sending cold shivers down my spine.

That, incidentally, was something the Confederates didn't actually do at Gettysburg. Not the sending cold shivers down my spine bit; I doubt giving me a few tingles would have been their priority given they were busy marching straight into the hugest and most concentrated blitz of firepower the world had ever seen. What they *didn't* do was screech the famous rebel yell, forbidden to do so on the day by their generals. No, the Confederate tactical plan at Gettysburg was simply to walk quietly uphill in a four-mile line and get shot. And it worked.

I watched in grim silence from the hilltop, throwing my CSA battle flag away in disgust as it became clear that the side I'd backed were mainly lying flat on their backs. I was also disgusted that I'd turned up at the wrong war. And further disgusted to discover that my parents listened to me even less than I listened to them. How could they have messed up so badly? They were out by two centuries and a continent.

So, in short, I was a thoroughly disgusted eight-year-old. But things changed very little. I still read everything I could find on our Civil War, still fought decisive battles on my bedroom floor (that's with toy soldiers – not fistfights with the cat or anything) and still marched around in a plastic helmet, albeit that of a

Roman legionary rather than an authentic Civil War soldier, pretending to be a Parliamentarian on the eve of Edgehill. One thing it did change, however, was my view on the literature available on our war.

The Confederate rout at Hemel had given me enough interest in the American Civil War to read up on that too. Whereas English Civil War books tended to be predominantly school-textbook affairs, getting rather too involved in the complicated political and religious aspects of the war and spending too little time on the battlefield, American books offered far more actual fighting and interesting trivia.

In short, they were exciting, whereas ours were not. Which brings me to a third reason for writing this book – I wanted to write one that *was*.

But I must confess that the main reason, the all-consuming primary reason, that I travelled up and down the country visiting every major Civil War battlefield, was through a terrible fear of my wife. Or rather, the fear that she would make good on a threat regarding my Civil War obsession.

Lorraine's words of solid encouragement on that fine Sunday morning still ring in my ears to this day: 'Either do the trip, write the flipping book, or it's a Civil War ban. I'm fed up with listening to it, on and on [and then mimicking me in a high-pitched whine], "I'm going to visit the battlefields, going to see what's there now, write a book, tell the story in a fun way" . . . WHEN? When are you doing that? It's been *ten* years – ten years of sitting in a call centre and writing the odd cat book. Do it now or all that "research stuff" (a whole room rendered unusable by piles of books, historical maps and prints) goes in the bin, and you never mention Cromwell again.'

'You can't do that . . . ' I countered, knowing she could and would. Her brows furrowed.

'I can and I will [told you so!]. Thinking about it, you can go with them because if you think I'm going to carry on financing this family while you earn peanuts . . . blah, blah, blah.'

From that point on, the blahs are all I remember of the conversation, some louder and more urgent than others, but mainly blahs. I'd drifted away. I was already planning my trip.

I knew deep down that she was right. It was time to stop talking, stop spending my days ringing hundreds of people from that call centre simply to annoy them, and write the book I'd always dreamed of writing. And if I didn't . . . well, she's a strong woman.

Armed with a new sense of resolve and purpose, I headed off to the Prince of Wales public house to drown it.

A lunchtime pint has long been my Sunday tradition. As usual I plonked myself down at the bar beside an old friend named Pete Ilic, a huge, loud, gentle giant, known to many, through reasons of poor name planning, as Pillock (P. Ilic). Actually, the description 'friend' would probably have to be used in a very loose way here. Certainly we drank together often, far too often, but I was never quite sure whether our friendship was based on actually liking one another, or on mutual hatred. Probably a little of both.

'Afternoon,' he bellowed, startling a nearby septuagenarian so badly that half her drink sloshed to the floor. 'Looking a bit thoughtful for a Sunday, aren't you?'

Taking a brief break from mental trip-planning, I told him of the morning's developments.

After a long pause, and an even longer gulp of beer, he wiped his mouth on the back of his sleeve and casually remarked, 'Sounds OK. We'll do it.'

'What? You? No! You're not coming! It's about book research. Why on earth would you come? You've no interest in the Civil War whatsoever. Every time I mention it, you tell me to "Shut it". No way are you coming.'

Within five minutes, he was coming, within ten he'd changed the entire purpose of the battlefield visits. No longer would we simply be visiting every major battlefield; we'd also be visiting every battlefield pub.

'I'm not sure, Pete. For one thing, there could be hundreds of pubs, how would we visit them all?'

'We'll manage. Anyway, you like the Civil War and beer . . . and I like beer. It has to be done.'

I sloshed back a mouthful of Brakspear's IPA, and realised he had a very good point. And also, a very good idea. Not just a Comical-Historical-Travelogue as planned, but now a Comical-Historical-Travelogue-Pub-Crawl. Hah! Let them categorise that! My last two books had been comedies too, but due to a cat being the star, the books were mistakenly filed in the 'Pets and Livestock' section of virtually every bookshop. This one would completely befuddle them! It really *did* have to be done. And it wasn't so very different from my original plan. I was still, at long last, going to visit the famous battlefields of the First English Civil War, to see for myself the sites of those incredibly momentous events, discover what now stood on that once scarred and bloody ground.

And I'd always wanted to come up with a lighter, less confused look at the Civil War than the old school textbooks served up. With the introduction of Pillock and a pub crawl, that look was getting lighter by the moment – a look that would hopefully enable the reader to, as the trip progressed, draw much fun and pleasure from the terrible death and destruction befalling others. Not quite the in-depth study I'd perhaps once intended to write, but instead, an incredibly shallow pub crawl through four years of bloody carnage. Perfect!

Three pints later we raised a half-cut pint to what Pete had already christened 'The Mission' and, suddenly, everybody in the pub stood and cheered. He'd been even louder than usual, it would seem.

And so, just like that, my quest began. Drink after drink came our way and a date was set for our first visit – to the famous battleground of Edgehill. I eventually staggered off home, blissfully happy and confident.

In the intervening, more sober, days, I wondered if I'd made the right choice. Pete and I were fine together during pub sessions, but we had an incredible ability to irritate each other when attempting to do anything else but sit at a bar.

Our whole friendship started with a row, in fact. Both working for a local courier company at the time, we'd been hand-picked as the two 'most unlikely to be missed', and sent on a gruelling five-day van-trek delivering boxes of leaflets to Madrid and Lisbon. I'm still not sure how we survived. Now, in more sensible days, we all of us tend to realise that driving all day long, drinking all night long, and then resuming your trip at dawn over foreign, often mountainous, roads doesn't really fit with any known Health and Safety guidelines, either for us or for anybody else on the road.

For five days, a wobbling Ford Transit hurtled through France, Spain and Portugal, the sounds of almost constant arguing emanating from within. We saw eye to eye on nothing . . . except perhaps the need to spend our entire hotel allowance on beer and sleep in the back of the van. It was this habit, in fact, that very nearly saw me arrested in Lisbon. We'd parked up outside our drop-off point and spent an uncomfortable night slumped over a pile of jagged boxes. At daybreak, I began going through the full repertoire of my daily hygiene ritual – cleaning my teeth. In the back of the now rather unpleasant-smelling van, I brushed thoroughly and rinsed my mouth with bottled water. I then shoulder-barged the van's very stiff ill-fitting back doors open, and spat out a huge mouthful of toothpaste and water.

For the woman it hit, it must have been a truly horrific moment. On a deserted street at 6 a.m., a van's back doors fly open to reveal a pale and unhealthy-looking young man clad only in dirty boxer shorts. The sheer shock of that sight hasn't even begun to sink in when he appears to summon up vast quantities of phlegm from absolutely nowhere, and showers you in it, so copiously that for a moment you can see nothing but white water. My attempts to apologise proved useless, particularly as she was running away and I appeared to be chasing her.

As was, I suppose, inevitable, she turned out to be the very person we were delivering to. We were, after all, parked just around the corner from her place of work, and she was probably the only person in all Lisbon asked to get in at 6 a.m. and receive leaflets from two half-drunken English vagrants.

I discovered this coincidence upon knocking on her door ten minutes later, only to have it slammed (understandably) shut in my face. Our attempts to explain the situation by shouting through her side window in a language she didn't understand only served to bring a squad car screeching to the scene. After some help with translation and a stern warning about spitting in people's faces, we were allowed to go on our way.

Much of the trip was like this. It ended with Pete getting so drunk on the overnight ferry home that he failed to make it back to our cabin. Indeed, the only trace of him at disembarkation time was his shoes, still facing the bar that he'd been standing at for most of the night. After a fruitless search beneath bar tables, I raced back to the cabin, packed our holdalls and made my way down to the car-deck, hoping that even if he'd forgotten his cabin number, he'd remember where the van was parked.

But there was no sign of him. I finally gave up and climbed into the driver's seat, assuming he'd probably just fallen overboard during the night and drowned, something simple like that. Then I found him. He was on the end of my arm.

Appearing suddenly, he wrenched open my door, grabbed my arm in a vice-like grip and hauled me out of the seat. Through his manic, drunk-beyond-drunken haze, the one thing he had remembered was that it was his turn to drive. This wasn't something I was about to let him do, and a struggle ensued. Pete's unco-ordinated attempts to grab the van keys led only to his becoming boggle-eyed and disorientated as I desperately juggled them from hand to hand.

Then, as suddenly as the scuffle started, it was over, Pete seemingly deciding he didn't want to go home in the van after all and running ashore with the foot passengers, hurling abuse at me over his shoulder as he went. We didn't see him again for three days.

It was with this man that I intended to spend a large amount of time travelling around England. As far as I could see, the omens weren't good.

Lorraine, on the other hand, welcomed the news that Pete would be accompanying me. 'Somebody to look out for you,' she said, and keep me focused. She really had no idea what she was saying. For one thing, Pete's focus was rarely stable.

As things were to turn out, many of my misgivings were well founded. In other ways, though, Pete was to prove invaluable.

For example, a vital part of my visits involved the interviewing of local people. You can pick up so much that is rarely found in textbook histories by simply talking to people. I discovered some fascinating local stories, verified by further research, that I'd entirely missed during thirty years of study. And these were the interesting bits. The bits concerning luckless coincidences, useless generals, sex-crazy earls, hauntings, exhumations, mysteries and the like.

For instance, it was in The Lamb in Chalgrove that I discovered that no bird or animal will ever set foot upon a quiet corner of Chalgrove Field, scene of a nasty skirmish in the summer of 1643. Birds won't even fly over the area. I strongly believed at the time that this story was aimed entirely at forcing me, in the name of research, to sit in a wet field for seven hours staring at . . . well, nothing really.

Absolutely nothing for hours. The story was true. I watched birds change direction in midair so many times I lost count. And all were avoiding the same patch of battlefield.

Snippets like this, discovered in a pub, provided me with the sort of tales from history and oddities that I love.

The need to interview was important, therefore. But I possess a relatively quiet nature. Not the sort to march up to someone and launch into a barrage of seemingly pointless questions. Pete, however, is. OK, so the vast majority of the 'local people' interviewed turned out to be semi-drunken pub dwellers, but that proved even better in many ways. My information-gathering techniques had been simplified immeasurably – I just sat my drunk with theirs. A seventeen-stone, booze-fuelled interviewing machine. And the atmosphere he could create was amazing. More often than not he had the whole pub talking, throwing war stories back and forth while I sat drinking beer and happily taking notes.

For that reason I'd like to dedicate this book to him.

But I won't.

Instead I will dedicate it to Charles I of England, without whom the English Civil War, and therefore this book, would probably not have been possible.

Annoying One's Subjects

In which the Author attempts to massively simplify the causes of a crazily complex war, and proves that 'simple' comes naturally

The introduction was easy. It concerned straightforward reasons for doing something, based on lifelong ambition and driven by a fear of loss, humiliation and divorce. Simple, basic and, I repeat, massively shallow reasons.

The causes of the English Civil War were not so straightforward. Complex politically, complex religiously and complex for the sake of being complex. These causes stretched back way before the actual outset of war in 1642, and originally concerned long-running divisions between the Protestant and Catholic Churches.

My main aim for this chapter was not to get bogged down in the massive quagmire of conflicting opinions and extensive data on why the war was fought, and to skip through it at breakneck speed to get to the fighting and the pubs. Hard-nosed historians please note, I intended to be grossly simplistic with this chapter and I think I've done rather well! Anyway, with all the aforementioned tension going on, King Charles I marrying Henrietta Maria, a French Catholic princess, in 1625 did little to please Protestant England. Neither did his issue of certain guidelines to the Church of England three years later – guidelines that seemed to prove that Charles had Catholic leanings. This was probably true. So in love with Henrietta Maria was he, that many believed he did most things simply to please her.

So, in the blue corner an under-the thumb king who, despite doing exactly as he was told by his wife, strongly believed that he could do exactly as he pleased with everybody else. And his wife agreed with him, for she and Charles believed in the 'divine right of kings'.

Somebody being convinced that he's absolutely (and divinely) right in everything he does would always be mildly irritating. But when that person decides the fate of the country's taxes, wars and religion, there's the possibility of trouble. And trouble there was. A political struggle ensued, culminating in Parliament passing three pretty serious resolutions, condemning any change in religion, condemning any taxation levied without their consent and declaring any merchant paying illegal taxes a traitor.

Knowing himself to be completely right about everything, Charles must have found being overruled something of a surprise, but he nevertheless took it well, angrily dismissing Parliament in 1629 and imprisoning three members of the Commons. As explanation for his actions he offered the statement, 'Princes are not bound to give account of their actions, but to God alone.'

Which although true of us all at the end of the

day, probably didn't help much. With that Charles pressed on with his reforms – unhindered by Parliament, which remained dissolved – raising new taxes, appointing an Archbishop of Canterbury with Catholic leanings of his own, and attempting to impose his guidelines on the Scottish Church.

You should never interfere with the Scottish. Exercise extreme caution if you intend interfering with a Scotsman in any Glasgow pub. The Scottish responded first by rioting, then by expelling all bishops installed in Scotland by Charles's father James I, and then by raising an army.

Enter at this stage one of the most fantastically unlucky men it has ever been my pleasure to read of. Thomas Wentworth, Earl of Strafford, had been busy bullying the Irish during Charles's reign of tyranny.

Having merrily brought Ireland to the brink of revolution with his 'firm hand' leadership, it was decided he had a way with the Celts, so Charles ordered him to go and sort Scotland out.

Wentworth wasn't daft. He realised that the army at his disposal wasn't going to be sufficient. His advice was the recall of Parliament, who could raise funds for a properly trained and equipped army. It was excellent advice and, as such, was totally ignored. Instead, Wentworth was sent north with a rubbish army that got soundly beaten as soon as it reached the border. His good advice was now accepted. In 1640 Parliament was recalled, agreed with the King on absolutely nothing and got dismissed again. Not for nothing is it remembered as the Short Parliament.

So the loyal and once-pummelled Wentworth

headed north again, with another makeshift collection of soldiers and the honourable intention of getting another Scottish kicking. But even this seemingly simple plan didn't go well. Wentworth's talent for upsetting people hadn't failed him since his departure from Ireland – his army mutinied and buggered off in all directions bar Scotland. The Scottish, fed up with waiting, marched south and occupied northern England. Just to rub Charles's nose in it, they then demanded Charles pay their army's occupation expenses.

Wentworth's original advice on Parliament's recall was again acted upon and – how unlucky is this? – one of the first acts of the new, new Parliament was to arrest Wentworth and have him beheaded for treason.

This really wasn't a bloke you'd like to sit next to on a light aeroplane, is it? The poor chap gets dragged across from Ireland to serve his king, has to ride all the way to Scotland on a horse twice – against his own sensible advice – getting beaten once and losing his army the second time, and then he gets executed for treason, being the first person in our history convicted of treason for the exact opposite of treason.

Parliament got busy. They passed Act after Act during 1640 and 1641, diminishing the power of the monarchy, abolishing Charles's favourite taxes, and effectively handing themselves control of everything worth controlling, including the country's defences. Ireland had by now moved into full revolt and the Scots were still occupying the North. Things were definitely looking a tad messy overall, so Parliament rounded things off by issuing a list of grievances against Charles, blaming him for absolutely everything. So how did Charles take all this? Thirteen years had passed since he'd arrested members of the Commons for speaking against him. Thirteen years is a very long time to reflect on earlier errors. Charles was now older and wiser, and he applied his new-found wisdom by ordering the arrest of members of the Commons who'd spoken against him. Two of these men were John Pym and John Hampden.

John Hampden features later in this book, not so much for what he did during the war – although brave and honourable by all accounts, his most notable involvement was getting himself fatally wounded during his first few minutes of battle – as for his part in bizarre events two centuries later.

Hampden's feud with Charles went back two decades. In 1626 he was imprisoned for refusing to lend Charles money. If we still had laws to that effect, I'd have had my parents put away years ago. Then, in 1635, Hampden was taken to court for refusing to pay a tax. The tax, named Ship Money, had previously been confined to coastal towns who paid for Royal Navy protection. In an effort to raise money, Charles suddenly decided the tax should be paid by inland towns too. Hampden, living in Buckinghamshire and surrounded by green hills, hadn't considered the possibility of a naval attack on his estate.

He was having none of it. He was taken to court and lost his case, but the public gave him such massive support that Charles found the tax uncollectable. Hampden was there again in 1640 leading the motion to oppose Charles's request for a Parliamentary grant to invade Scotland, and therefore causing the dismissal of the aforementioned

Short Parliament. By now Charles must have realised that if there was one thing John Hampden didn't like, it was giving him money. For all this Hampden earned himself the title Pater Patriae – the father of the people. It was little surprise that Charles wasn't keen on him.

Neither was John Pym one to whom Charles would have sent a birthday card, for it was Pym who finally moulded Parliament into a revolutionary force. It was he who smoothed out the differences between those fighting a political campaign and those fighting a religious one. It was Pym who made it possible for Parliament to stand as one against the King. Winston Churchill later proclaimed Pym as the very heart of the Roundhead war. And if John Hampden's honorary title hadn't been enough to wind Charles up, then John Pym's nickname of 'King Pym' must have been.

By 1642, Parliament *had* become wiser – they refused to recognise the charges made against their own. Charles wasn't going to leave it there. He nipped down to the House of Commons with a troop of horsemen and swordsmen to arrest the accused men, who had already received warning and fled. 'I see the birds have flown,' Charles famously said to a nervous Commons, no doubt stroking his baddie beard menacingly.

If the country hadn't already been on a war footing, this act of aggression put it firmly so. Charles instantly became more than a little unpopular, particularly in London. As people all around him began stating their loyalty to Parliament, it was Charles's turn to flee the capital, taking his family from Whitehall and moving to nearby Hampton Court.

Through all of this, Charles and Parliament kept negotiations going, but neither side was giving an inch and both were busily mobilising. In January 1642, Charles's wife Henrietta Maria headed for Europe to rally Catholic assistance, toting the Crown Jewels, which she intended to swap for arms. In March, Parliament took control of the country's militia, and in April Charles and his followers marched to Hull to gather arms stashed after the successful 'upset Scotland campaigns'. Marching north went as well as ever – his way was blocked by a hastily raised Parliamentary naval and land force. So Charles skirted Hull and marched to York, where he set up HQ.

By summer both sides had stocked up on arms and ammunition and gathered sufficient numbers of men willing to be butchered in some lonely field. Two opposing English armies stood ready to fight. Parliament lit the fuse – issuing Charles with a list of nineteen propositions.

If, as Parliament claimed, 'The Nineteen Propositions' were actually an attempt on their part to avoid all-out war, then not much effort was wasted. The propositions basically called for Parliamentary power over everything. Parliament made it clear that they were quite happy for Charles to remain King Charles, just so long as he didn't do any kinging.

There was no way Charles was ever going to accept that. On 22 August 1642, King Charles I raised his Royal Standard at Nottingham and declared war on Parliament. The bloodiest war ever to be fought on British soil had begun.

The Muddy Ground – The Battle of Edgehill

In which England begins the task of visiting terrible destruction upon itself, and the Author visits terrible destruction upon a pub carpet

I arrived at Edgehill on an October day, much as almost 30,000 soldiers had 360-odd years before me – tired, fed up and wanting to kill someone. In my case, it was my travelling companion Pete. An hour and a half's crawl up the M40 motorway had taken its toll on him. He'd been promised a pub or two, not this. He also had a niggling suspicion that I'd been totally lost for the last half-hour, and that when I finally worked out where the battlefield was supposed to be, I'd probably want to go and stand in it. That being the type of weird thing I do.

And he was right on all three counts. Yes, I was lost, yes, I wanted to stand in an empty field, and yes, that's weird. I finally pulled into a muddy lay-by and studied my battle map. I stared long and hard at the rather sketchy details of the two armies' deployment. I then stared bewildered at the high hedges all around me. No matter where I'd driven, all I'd seen were hedges. No road signs saying 'Huge Great Battlefield – Straight Ahead', no brown tourist boards, no 'Entry to Battlefield' barrier and kiosk containing the obligatory miserable attendant. Nothing. Just empty lanes, cold drizzle and hedges.

'You seen everything you need to see, then?' asked Pete.

'What? We've only been here half an hour. How can I have seen "everything"? I've seen nothing. Except bloody hedges!'

Bitter silence resumed.

I put the car in first and had begun to pull away when Pete helpfully wrenched the handbrake full on. Carefully removing my nose from the steering wheel, I stared blankly at him. He could be unpredictable at the best of times, but this was a new one. A mental picture of a possible handbrake-turn on the M40 en-route home flashed across my mind.

But Pete was solemnly pointing straight ahead. I strained my eyes through the drizzle. A monument! A small monument. Just feet from the car. I'd been about to drive past it. I jumped out of the car, my spirits soaring, took two steps forward and slipped flat on my face into six inches of soggy mud.

I lay perfectly still for a few moments, reflecting on the sheer joy of living. After a few abortive attempts to lift myself from the incredibly slippery ground I crawled back to the car and grabbed the door handle, using it as a lever with which to pull myself up. Clambering up the side of the car, muddy hands struggling for grip against the wet window, I involuntarily looked in at Pete. He was staring straight ahead. He glanced towards me, jumped considerably at the unexpected mud-splattered apparition clawing at now filthy windows, and then resumed his solemn monument-staring.

Regaining my composure slightly but failing miserably to look dignified, I slipped and stumbled my way to the monument. I wondered briefly at the small cross and wreaths laid before it. Who was laying wreaths here? Wreaths to soldiers who'd died over three centuries before?

I read the monument's inscription:

BETWEEN HERE AND THE VILLAGE
OF RADWAY THE BATTLE OF
EDGEHILL, THE FIRST OF THE CIVIL
WAR, WAS FOUGHT ON SUNDAY THE
23 OCTOBER 1642. MANY OF THOSE
WHO LOST THEIR LIVES IN THE
BATTLE ARE BURIED THREE
QUARTERS OF A MILE TO THE
SOUTH OF THIS STONE.

As a memorial, it was straight to the point and poignant. As a gravestone, it had missed by three quarters of a mile.

I slid back to the car and slopped into my seat.

Pete seemed to have brightened considerably during my five-minute absence. Probably because of my five-minute absence.

'Right,' he exclaimed, rubbing his hands together. 'We'd better get to the pub, it took a lifetime getting here, didn't it?'

'It was an hour and a half's drive – that's all! Why are you here, Pete? I mean . . . why?'

'I'm on a Mission.'

'Yes, yes, but you've no interest at all. This isn't going to work out, is it? After today, I'm doing the visits on my own.'

'Can't let you do that, mate.'

'Why, because of the *Mission*?'

'Yeah. Well, that and the fact I took two hundred quid in bets after you rolled home.'

'What? Bets on what? With who?'

'The landlord, barman, regulars – they all bet we won't visit every pub. They reckon I won't bother, there'll be too many pubs, and you never stick with anything.'

Charming. And such unfair criticism. Maybe I *had* failed to complete (or sometimes even start) around twenty projects in the last few years, while tending to flit between jobs, and maybe I did now spend most of my time in a call centre but . . . well, OK, so it was completely fair criticism. Even worse though, Pete now had a vested interest.

'Are we going to the pub now, or not?'

'Yes, fine,' I huffed.

'Great, you'd better clean yourself up a bit, then. You look like you just fought the ruddy battle yourself!'

With that he sat chuckling to himself all the way to the Castle Inn at the top of Edge Hill, where I would soon discover something deeply annoying.

And on the subject of annoying, Pete's constant whingeing at the sheer epicness of his short car journey to Edgehill would no doubt have made him the target of quite a few angry pikes, muskets, staffs and swords, had the poor combatants of the battle heard him at it, as the majority had had to walk there. And quite a route they'd taken as well.

You see, the sides had done a lot of marching following the declaration of war in August.

Loads of marching – much of it simply for the joy of marching. Up and down the country they went . . . marching.

Between marches both armies, initially boasting only around 15,000 men between them, captured this town or that town, peeving many inhabitants but gradually raising their numbers through local support. That support was split and confused. There were no definite geographical loyalties. Royalist support tended to centre around Wales and the north and west of England, while the richer south and east of England were often for Parliament. Many major cities, including London, were in the hands of Parliament, whilst Charles was popular in rural communities.

But even that confused picture is oversimplifying things, because the situation could differ from village to village, wherever in the country you lived. Neither was the English Civil War a class struggle. Just as many titled gentlemen fought for Parliament as for the King. As many commoners fought for the King as for Parliament. Just to emphasise how personal loyalties were from man to man, and also to confuse matters further, at one point during the war there were more members of the two houses of Parliament with the King than there were at Westminster.

So, utterly muddled and zigzagging relentlessly, the armies of King and Parliament somehow came to meet one another at Edgehill.

The Royalists had marched from Shrewsbury. Having been in the East Midlands two months previously, and now heading to London from the extreme west of England, you can grasp just how much these people enjoyed walking.

Headed by King Charles, the army's most interesting commander on the day was a man for whom the term 'Cavalier' could have been invented – meet Prince Rupert. Cavalier in dashing appearance, cavalier in attitude. Twenty-two years old at the start of hostilities, Rupert seemed to like fighting very much. Indeed, he'd been fighting in Europe's Thirty Years' War when he heard his Uncle Charles was starting a war of his own.

He was home in a jiffy, eager to assist Charles in any way he could and hopefully find lots of new people to kill. He proved a valuable asset to the Royalist cause at the start of the war, capably commanding the Royalist cavalry and possessing more military know-how than Charles and most of his advisors put together. It would seem he massively enjoyed it all. At Edgehill, it was reported that he couldn't wait to get started, preferring to 'fight than eat'. This enthusiasm to get straight in there and scrap it out would prove on some occasions advantageous and on others damaging.

The Parliamentarians, meanwhile, had been ordered to halt Charles's army before it reached London, and headed out from Worcester under Robert Devereux, the Third Earl of Essex. Given what we now know about this man's military prowess and incredible leadership, it is little wonder that Essex marched parallel to Charles's army all the way to Warwickshire without ever knowing it was there.

Essex had started as he meant to go on. He had a true ability for the dazzlingly useless. And it seems it may have been a family trait. His father, the Second Earl of Essex and also called Robert, had been a favourite of Queen Elizabeth. As such, she had him executed.

But not without reason. In his early military career he was certainly brave. Romantically brave by many accounts. But in the two years preceding his death, you would have to say he was truly 'asking for it'. Despite (surprise, surprise) a military disaster in Ireland, which ended with his signing an unwanted and unauthorised truce with Irish rebels and deserting his own army, he was somehow allowed to keep his head on for a while.

Using it to the best of his ability while he still had it, he decided to incite an entirely futile and unworkable rebellion against the Queen. The only fighting that took place was a mini-riot during his own arrest. This time they took his head off for his own good. I think he'd probably finished with it anyway.

And so, with the inherited military tact and

cleverness of his father, the Third Earl of Essex took command of the Parliamentary army. It's a good job he did from my point of view. The war would probably have been over a lot sooner without him. We may well never have seen many of the great battles that were to come. But Essex played a vital role. It wasn't that he was there just to give the Royalists a sporting chance or anything – it just sometimes seemed like it. In fairness to Essex, the Royalists had little idea of the Parliamentarian's position either. Not until the day prior to the battle, at least. Only the chance capture of a group of opposition troops on 22 October gave them the information they needed. Knowing that their enemy was based around the village of Kineton, the Royalists marched to face them.

On the morning of 23 October 1642, the Royalist army arrived at the top of Edge Hill.

And the top of Edge Hill was exactly where Pete and I were now, running from car park to pub door through a sudden downpour. As Pete hurtled into the pub in a state of 'almost taste the beer' frenzy, I stopped in the rain and stared at a sign above the Castle Inn door.

I'd read a couple of accounts of the battle that claimed Charles had planned his army's deployment from this very inn. If these claims were true, he'd have had the huge benefit of hindsight. The sign showed quite clearly that the inn had been built in 1747, 105 years after the Battle of Edgehill. Never mind, I thought, stepping into the warm of the lounge bar and having a pint of Hook Norton Bitter shoved into my hand. I took a deep swig and then noticed that the landlady was staring at me in something approaching horror.

The Castle Inn has standards, I'm sure. I'm also sure that I fell well below them. Whilst a couple of travel wipes had sorted out my hands and face, my jeans and coat were still smothered in mud. Not only that, the sudden soaking I'd just received outside had diluted some dried mud I wasn't even aware of. Parallel rivulets of brown water were cascading down my face. Worst of all, I'd trailed mud everywhere. I backed to the door and removed my filth-encrusted shoes. The landlady never took her eyes off me, not for a moment.

By the time I'd tidied myself up a little in the toilets and returned for a second mouthful of beer, Pete had finished his first pint, and was moving swiftly on to a pint of Old Hooky. The man was on a mission. The landlady's attitude seemed to have softened towards me somewhat, as she shot me a quick smile, although it might have been a grimace. She liked Pete though, and the two chatted happily as I glanced around the room.

The word 'impressive' doesn't really do the Castle Inn justice. It's actually quite amazing.

For a start, it's exactly what it says on the label – it's completely castle-shaped, with two imposing towers. I'd seen the larger of the two towers from miles off, from the other side of the battlefield in fact.

Its own boast of being one of the most unusual inns in England is completely confirmed on first sight. The interior is just as eye-catching. A fire blazed to the right of the bar, above it an imposing painting of Prince Rupert, galloping into battle, sword above head. On the mantelpiece sat an ornamental Civil War cannon. And it didn't stop there. The room was positively littered with Civil War memorabilia. The walls were covered in battle maps, muskets, breastplates, battle paintings and portraits. A helmet stood mounted in a small alcove. The place is truly a Civil War wonderland. I wandered through to the public bar, which boasted yet more of the same, albeit with a rather out-of-place pool table plonked in among it all.

As I walked back into the lounge bar, my senses reeling with Civil War overload, my attention was stolen somewhat by the conversation at the bar. I half-caught the tail-end of Pete's last sentence, which seemed to be something along the lines of 'It's a shame when they stop caring like that. There's nothing you can do with them.' I don't know exactly what Pete had told the landlady, but she now seemed to be staring at me with sympathy rather than chagrin. Indeed, as I stepped back to the bar, her approach towards her muddiest ever customer was almost motherly.

I know the question was purely a business one, but there was something in the way she asked, 'Will you be eating today?' that made me think she assumed eating was something I hadn't bothered with in a while. She seemed genuinely surprised when we ordered two curries.

As she disappeared with our food order, Pete took a huge swig of Old Hooky and nodded towards a point somewhere on the far wall. I looked over my shoulder. He'd probably picked about the only bit of wall with nothing on it.

'What?' I enquired.

'There,' he answered, nodding again.

I turned around and stared at the blank piece of wall.

'What?' I repeated.

'There. Outside.'

Ah, he was nodding beyond the wall. How stupid of me to allow a solid wall to block my field of vision. Pete took another gulp of beer and pushed his glass forward, ready for a refill.

Quite what was beyond the wall wasn't forthcoming.

'Yes?' I ventured. 'Beyond the wall? What about it?'

'Oh,' he said, 'yeah, there's a balcony out there. You can see the whole battlefield. And there's a load of pamphlets on the bar telling you where everything happened. Beats me why you didn't just come up here in the first place. Told you we should've come straight to the pub. Always come straight to the pub. Remember that.'

I picked up the booklets and began reading. The first dealt with the inn itself, and particularly its tower. Building had started on the larger of the two towers in 1742, to commemorate the hundredth anniversary of the battle. It was opened eight years later, on the anniversary of Oliver Cromwell's death. It marks the very spot where Charles raised his standard and surveyed the battlefield.

The second booklet was a guide to the battlefield. I took it with me, walked through a door to the side of the bar, down a thin corridor and out onto a gazeboed ledge. Before me, the whole wide plain spread away into the distance. The Castle Inn may yet to have been built when the Civil War began, but this was surely the best point Charles could have chosen to survey the lay of the land.

We were on the very summit of Edgehill, which apart from being a small village is also a long ridge, dropping off to plains either side. Charles would have seen everything from up here. No wonder he chose this spot.

Which indeed begged the question as to why I hadn't. Why had I meandered aimlessly along drizzly lanes down there on the plain for half an hour, seeing nothing and falling over? Why hadn't I come here, had a pint, made use of the guidebooks, surveyed the battlefield and made my plans? Deeply annoying, to say the least. That's why Charles was a king and I've spent the last five years in a call centre, I suppose.

I scanned the field, sipping bitter and cheering up. It was awe-inspiring, almost breathtaking, to think what had happened down there over three and a half centuries before.

The Royalists had soon moved down the side of the hill on which I now stood, taking up battle positions along its base. Prince Rupert's cavalry regiments took up position on the right of the field, with further cavalry deploying on the left. Beyond the cavalry on both sides of the field were regiments of dragoons. In the centre were the infantry, numbering somewhere in the region of 10,000 men.

Parliament deployed in much the same manner, infantry in the centre, flanked by cavalry with musketeers on the extreme flanks, but with another two regiments of cavalry lying behind the infantry.

Essex had one plan in mind for the opening of the battle. He didn't want to start it. Therefore, inevitably, he started it. With 30,000 soldiers gathered on the field, it was quite clear that this was going to be a huge confrontation – the first large-scale hostilities of the war. Without doubt, this battle was going to be big news, and politically it was in Parliament's interest not to fire the first shots of the first major battle, and possibly the last battle as far as many were concerned at the time. Essex thought it essential that he should wait for the Royalists to make the first move. With this sound reasoning in mind he allowed the Royalists to deploy unhindered, even though in range of his artillery. Then, all of a sudden, sound reasoning went completely out of his head, and he opened fire.

Quite why is still unknown. All that is clear is that he suddenly pounded the enemy with cannon fire. There are various theories, one being that the artillery opened up without his actual order, and another that he'd spotted Charles and his advisors trotting across the Royalist lines and just couldn't resist shooting at them.

Whatever the reason, the most immediate effect of Essex's opening fire was Charles trotting back quite quickly whence he'd come, under the advice of his officers. Next, the Royalist artillery returned fire. Suddenly the field became a cauldron of deafening noise and billowing smoke.

Through the thunder of cannon, the dragoons and musketeers on both flanks of the battlefield waded into one another. After a brief fight, it was the Royalists, left and right, who came out on top, driving their Parliamentarian counterparts into retreat. Prince Rupert's cavalry took full advantage on the right, charging forward and cutting down Parliament's fleeing musketeers.

The opposing Roundhead cavalry rushed forward to assist their musketeers, but their resistance was short-lived, wilting under the sheer ferociousness of Rupert's attack. As quickly as they'd galloped forward, they were forced to retreat, leaving the poor musketeers to the mercy of Royalist swords. On the left wing too, the Royalist cavalry overcame their opposing numbers. Things were looking decidedly good for King Charles.

In the centre of the field, the two huge bodies of infantry came together with a metallic crash. Initially Parliament fared no better here than they had on the flanks. With the disasters befalling their cavalry and musketeers very much on their mind, one Parliamentarian regiment broke lines and fled. For a few harrowing moments, it looked as though the entire Parliamentarian line was about to break. But it didn't. Despite the loss of an entire regiment, the rest of the infantry stayed put and stubbornly held their ground. Soon both infantries were locked in stalemate, pushing pike against pike in the centre of the field.

And then things went horribly wrong for the Royalists. Their cavalry regiments' brakes had failed. When they'd won on the flanks they just carried on going, and going, and going. Instead of staying to support their infantry, they'd raced forward to plunder what they could from Parliamentarian supplies at the village of Kineton.

And so now, an unhindered Parliamentarian cavalry reserve, positioned behind their own infantry, came into their own, ploughing into the unprotected Royalist infantry.

Suddenly the Royalist lines buckled and broke. Parliamentarian infantry surged forward into the wide-open gaps.

Essex saw a possibility of victory, snatched from the jaws of defeat. More and more Roundhead foot soldiers were ordered forward. From a promising opening, the day was turning extremely ugly for the King's forces.

Somewhere off in the distance the Royalist cavalry finally stopped and decided that they'd probably best get back to the battle. If they'd delayed any longer, they'd have returned to a field already lost. But they were just in time, charging through the Parliamentarian rear, scattering infantry and cavalry alike, and allowing their own infantrymen to shore up gaps and reshape.

It was all square again. As darkness fell, the armies withdrew, both ending up exactly where they'd started the day. One or two thousand dead soldiers, and nobody had got anywhere.

Parliament held the better side of the field. While the Royalist soldiers, exhausted and hungry, had to be content with an uncomfortable night on the side of Edge Hill, the Parliamentarians at least had Kineton to withdraw to.

There is little of the present-day village of Kineton that resembles the Kineton of that fateful seventeenth-century day. Firstly, there are no wounded and dying Parliamentarian soldiers littering the streets – this was one of the first things Pete and I noticed on arrival there, although neither of us mentioned their absence.

Secondly, most buildings from the days of the civil war are gone. In old Kineton's place is a moderately pleasant little village. We drove up and down the two wide main streets, and all around the not-at-all-wide back streets. The village centre consists of a beautiful church, two pubs, a fish 'n' chip takeaway, half a dozen small shops and a memorial to those who died in the two World Wars. The church is truly impressive, while Kineton itself has a 'lived in' feel, not in the slightest touristy.

But it wasn't really Kineton that had my full attention at this moment. No, my senses had been overwhelmed by an appalling problem with Pete's guts. A pint of Hook Norton Bitter, three pints of Old Hooky and a pint of Hook Norton Dark accompanied by a spicy pub curry were having a dramatic effect on my passenger's constitution. Whether a foul green mist could be seen escaping my open windows as I drove along that day, I don't know. All I knew at the time was that I had to get out of the car, and fast. My eyes were watering, my stomach retching and I hardly dared breathe. We pulled up outside the Carpenter's Arms and I stumbled gagging from the car door. Pete, blissfully inebriated and seeing his foul series of 'episodes' en route as a thing to be celebrated rather than a problem, merrily followed me into the public bar, hands in pockets and humming a happy tune.

The Carpenter's Arms is a cosy little beamed pub, consisting of a warm and friendly carpeted lounge bar dominated by its fireplace, and a wooden-floored, two-tabled public bar with TV, fruit machine and dartboard.

The lounge bar was by far the more attractive of the two rooms. We chose the public bar.

We each had our own reasons for this. In Pete's case it was a sudden urge to play darts, while my decision was based entirely on the fact that the public bar was empty and if Pete was about to unleash anything like he'd inflicted on me in the car, then a room devoid of people was the place to do it.

For the moment, however, Pete was odour free and rubbing his hands with glee at the range of beers on offer. With Old Hooky, Adnams Southwold and Everards Tiger to choose from, there was every likelihood he'd go for all three. And he did.

After the first two pints and a disastrously long game of '301' that was still showing no signs of ending, Pete decided he'd interview the young(ish) barmaid. This was a strange decision, because the barmaid had so far proved unwilling to speak at all. A constant succession of incoming and outgoing mobile-phone text messages had her complete attention and the most she'd offered as yet was the odd nod and requests for various sums of cash.

Pete ambled to the bar, explaining that his colleague was an author and researching a book.

The barmaid glanced up from her phone. 'Is he famous?' she asked.

'No, but . . . '

'What's his name?'

'Chris Pascoe. He's on a Mission.'

'A what? Never heard of him. What books has he done?'

'*A Cat Called Birmingham* was his first . . . '

'You what?'

'*A Cat Called–*'

'Never heard of it.'

With that she was back punching keys and squinting at her phone screen. I stood by the dartboard hoping Pete would end it there. Instead, he went for another tack.

'What phone you got?'

The barmaid lit up like Blackpool Illuminations. A dramatic, animated five-minute phone comparison ensued. Finally Pete went for gold.

'Do you get many tourists in here, then?'

'Tourists? No. Why?'

'Well, you know, what with the battlefield being here and that.'

'Who'd come to this crummy town?'

He was losing her, I could see; her head was dipping towards her mobile.

'I'm surprised you don't play on the tourist angle a bit.'

Silence.

'Do you know much about the Civil War yourself?'

With a sudden unexpected intensity she looked Pete straight in the eye and said, 'You'll get nothing out of me!'

What? Did she think we were interrogating her? Did she perhaps believe that the Civil War had been a localised thing that she wasn't permitted to talk to 'outsiders' about? Or maybe that the war was still going on and that Pete and I were enemy spies?

Pete looked over at me and shrugged. The beep of mobile buttons resumed behind the bar, and Pete returned to take his turn at double-one. With all three darts missing the board by some way, it was obvious Pete's huge capacity for beer had almost been reached. But we had one more pub to go.

Leaving the Carpenter's Arms with a cheery wave, and hearing nothing but a Nokia ringtone in reply, we stepped back outside into the cold autumn drizzle. I walked across the road to the Swan Hotel, Pete stumbling and weaving happily behind me like a golden retriever, from lamp-post to litter bin to kerb.

The thing that had really struck me in the Carpenter's Arms, apart from one or two of Pete's darts, had been the total lack of anything Civil War. There'd been nothing. The walls had been full of small paintings and prints but almost all had depicted blood sports. There was shooting and cock-fighting aplenty, but no Civil War reference at all. I hoped the Swan Hotel would be different.

Within moments of walking through the door of the Swan, vaguely aware of Pete crashing straight into it just behind me, I could see it was the same story. In fact the two pubs are quite alike in many ways. The same small cosy lounge bar and beamed ceilings, the same games and TV-orientated public bar, and the same total lack of acknowledgement of the huge battle that had taken place outside their doors. Maybe my theory on the reluctance of the Carpenter's Arm's barmaid to discuss the war had been correct after all. Maybe there really was a 'don't mention the war' attitude in this town.

The Swan is larger than the Carpenter's Arms and most of the extra space is used up in the public bar, which is split between the aforementioned games area, and a large fireside array of tables and chairs.

The main difference between the Swan and the Carpenter's that day was that the Swan had lots of people in it. And the majority of those at the bar were very much in the same condition as Pete, who very quickly became one of their group.

Something akin to a party atmosphere began to spark up behind me as I studied the pub's walls. When Pete gets merry, merry is the word. And his new friends seemed completely up for some merriment. 'Old Hooky all round!' came a shout, followed by a huge raucous cheer.

I stepped up to the bar, looked longingly at the Old Hooky pump but walked away with my Diet Coke to continue wall-staring. Nothing. No Civil War prints at all. Just more shooting, hunting and baiting. In fact, it seemed that the standard criterion to be met if you're a pub painting in Kineton is that you must depict some kind of unpleasantness for animals.

Indeed, I saw only a couple of prints that didn't live up to this, and one of those involved a pig bathing in a pond – probably hung on the wall under the mistaken impression that it was drowning. If it had been a Kineton pig in a pond, I have little doubt that someone would have been along to drown it before too long anyway.

The atmosphere at the bar had progressed into a good-natured row, and the subject was now the Battle of Edgehill, completely smashing my unlikely 'secrecy theory' to bits. Pete's suggestion that the two lovely 'olde worlde' country pubs of Kineton should be transformed into Civil War 'theme pubs' didn't seem to be getting a sympathetic hearing. The 'clockwork Roundheads' and 'pub garden fairground rides' ideas were being met with particularly vehement opposition. The general opinion in the pub seemed to be that nobody was in the slightest bit interested in the Civil War, and perhaps the thing that most significantly bore this out for me was a leaflet dispenser in the games area.

You see these things in many pubs, particularly in tourist towns and seaside resorts; a big bank of leaflets advertising local museums, places of interest, art galleries, dinosaur worlds, theme parks, the works. Of all the many leaflets at the Swan Hotel, covering all of the aforementioned and more, not one leaflet had anything to do with the Battle of Edgehill or the English Civil War.

Turning from the rack in mild disbelief, I glanced out of the window and noticed that the store opposite was a gun shop, catering for all our hunting needs. Kineton certainly seems to know what it likes. I returned to the bar, and sat on a stool alongside a now permanently grinning Pete.

'So who won the battle, then?' asked Pete suddenly, giving my face a liberal coating of dry-roasted peanuts. 'Was it a draw?'

'Yeah,' I replied, wiping my eyes, half-blinded with salt. 'More or less. The Royalists claimed a victory because the Parliamentarians withdrew to Warwick rather than fight on the next day, but it was all pretty inconclusive. The main thing was that Essex took the Parliamentarians out of the King's way, so the Royalists could have marched straight on to take London, which was what they wanted to do in the first place.'

'Oh, did they do that, then?'

'No.'

'Why not? MORE OLD HOOKY OVER HERE PLEASE, LOVE, AND ANOTHER BAG OF DRY ROASTED!'

While Pete ordered his pint and his cronies cheered the arrival of another round, I mulled that question over. It was one of history's turning points. Had the King marched on an unprotected London, he could possibly have gone on to win the war. But instead, the Royalists wasted lots of time on a pillaging and plundering spree. By the time an understrength body of the Royalist army reached London, Essex's army had returned to block him.

And it wasn't only Essex that barred the way. London militias, concerned at news of Royalist pillaging and not wanting to be pillaged, had mobilised in force and joined the Parliamentarians at Brentford. The Royalists had a look at what was facing them and even Prince Rupert didn't fancy it.

They turned and left, burning a few things, nicking this and that and sinking the odd boat on the Thames as they went, a great chance to take London wasted before they'd even arrived.

A face full of peanuts and a disconcerting rumble of guts brought me back to reality. Pete raised his glass to me and toasted Kineton. He'd completely forgotten the question so I didn't bother with the answer. I rapped glasses, almost falling backwards off my stool in the face of Pete's overenthusiastic force. Kineton was indeed a nice village, but not if you're a Civil War buff. Or a pheasant.

Half an hour later we left Kineton and headed for the motorway, a 30mph tin can of gut-wrenchingly renewed foul air and radio-karaoke singing. I reflected that, if I was to ever finish this Mission, I'd be requiring the patience of a saint, earplugs, peanut-proof eyewear and a nose peg. I made a mental note to check a few army surplus websites for a gas mask to cover half of my requirements, but then instantly changed my mind when considering the long-lasting trauma this could cause any driver pulling up alongside a Citroen C2 occupied by a wildly animated fat man and a sinister-looking psycho in a World War Two gas mask.

And so Edgehill receded into the distance, but I'd soon be back. The Battle of Edgehill may have finished that day in 1642, but it hadn't quite finished with the village of Kineton.

By early 1643 Kineton had become the most haunted village in England.

A Dark Night on Edgehill

In which the Author bravely attempts to confront the supernatural, but instead appears to urinate over himself in a public house

A few nights later, I was back at Edgehill, alone.

The combined forces of King and Parliament couldn't have prised Pillock from his fireside seat at our Buckinghamshire local, the Prince of Wales, that blustery evening. But the day was 23 October, the anniversary of the battle, and something odd sometimes happens at Edgehill on 23 October. I had to be there, on that night, back in those dark country lanes . . . listening.

Because the Battle of Edgehill may have taken place in 1642, but it's happened again since. By many accounts, it's still happening, and it would have to be said that Edgehill is as ghostly a place as you could hope to find in our overly haunted country.

Spectral activity was first witnessed just a couple of months after the battle, in December 1642, and soon became big national news. The earliest available information can be found in a 1643 London pamphlet entitled *A Great Wonder in Heaven*, which describes a ghostly battle fought in the sky over Edgehill. The pamphlet states that shepherds, countrymen and travellers witnessed 'the late apparitions and prodigious noise of war and battles seen on Edge-Hill'.

The event apparently occurred on the Saturday before Christmas 1642, almost two months after the original battle, and began some time between midnight and 1 a.m. It all started with some startlingly loud sound effects. Witnesses could clearly hear the beat of drums, clash of arms and the groans of dying men. So real were these sounds that everyone thought a new battle was under way.

Well, you would, wouldn't you? Very few would automatically think, 'That's not a real battle. That'll just be a thousand ghosts fighting.'

The aforementioned shepherds, countrymen and travellers followed their ears and rushed to see what was happening. But the field was empty.

Suddenly, visuals joined sound effects. The ghostly image of a battle refought appeared in the sky above. For almost three hours the terrified witnesses cowered in fear as Parliamentarians and Royalists clashed once again, but this time the combatants who fought to the death were two months dead already, so in no immediate danger.

As suddenly as it had all started, it was over. Edgehill fell silent.

A shocked audience, finally daring to move, got up and ran all the way to Kineton, knocking up the village dignitaries and telling their amazing tale. Quite what these dignitaries thought about being woken at four in the morning by a madly jabbering group of men in soiled underwear isn't recorded. But it seems that, presumably once the jabberers had proved they hadn't just got back from a mega booze-up over in Radway, they were taken seriously. For the very next night, the dignitaries themselves, along with many other villagers, went to the battlefield. Most were soon returning, absolutely horrified, to their homes.

It's likely that many thought they were off on a jolly little countryside jaunt and that nothing at all would happen. However, shortly after midnight a huge volley of cannon fire, followed no doubt by a huge volley of stunned gasps, preceded another three hours of frenzied activity. The ghosts were really on form this night. Drums and trumpets replaced the roar of cannon as spectres appeared in the sky once more, charging across Edgehill to fight their equally spectral adversaries.

By morning, Kineton was a village in shock. Nobody knew quite what to do about it all.

What could you do? There was talk of taking word to King Charles, but Monday was a quiet night, completely devoid of phantom Parliamentarians and chilling Cavaliers.

Tuesday, Wednesday, Thursday and Friday all passed without the slightest hint of ghostly gunfire or sword-swinging spirits. Why alert Royalty to the fact the village had apparently gone crazy when it appeared to be over? But it wasn't over. It was about to get much, much worse.

On Saturday night, the battle began again, but this time the noise was so loud it woke the entire village. And the battle was even longer, continuing for almost four hours through the night. Some shocked and sleep-deprived inhabitants decided it was all too much, left their homes and fled the village. When the battle repeated yet again on Sunday night, it was decided something had to be done. The village's minister took word to King Charles, who had now set up headquarters in Oxford (presumably getting there in a wild, zig-zagging, pillaging motion).

Typically, the field now fell silent. But it still wasn't over. On 4 January 1643, the village was awoken in the dead of night by, according to the London pamphlet, 'the doleful and hideous groans of dying men crying revenge'. These sounds weren't carrying from the battlefield. They were emanating from Kineton's own streets. Then, drums and trumpets sounded 'as if an enemy had entered their town'. While most villagers lay shivering with fear in their beds, those who dared to peep through their windows saw groups of ghostly horsemen 'riding one against the other'.

The ghosts had come to town. To the great relief of Kineton, they didn't stay long, suddenly vanishing into thin air and leaving a deeply disturbed village behind them.

King Charles, meanwhile, was intrigued by the information he'd received from Kineton's minister. Certain that he himself hadn't been back to Edgehill, fighting every weekend, and equally sure that Rupert hadn't been sneaking out at night, Charles dispatched a group of officers to investigate. They got a lot more detail than they could have expected, or wanted.

These men, having fought at Edgehill themselves, were understandably horrified to see the whole terrible battle spark up again before their eyes, and even more horrified to see colleagues and friends, known to have perished, taking part in the grisly action, among them one Sir Edmund Verney. Sir Edmund had been the King's standard-bearer on the day of the battle.

When captured by Parliamentarians, he'd refused steadfastly to hand over the standard. The Parliamentarians understood his position and were sympathetic, cutting his hand off and killing him. In the to and fro of battle, the standard eventually found its way back into Royalist hands. Royalist hands in more ways than one. Sir Edmund's hand was still attached to the standard. This steadfast act of loyalty and bravery had been a talking point ever since his death. Since his *death*. And yet here he was, fighting in the sky over Edgehill, engaging in hand-to-hand combat to the amazement of his old brothers-in-arms.

Excuse the puns.

The King's shaken officers confirmed that Kineton did indeed have a ghost problem, but could do nothing but take word to Charles, who had far too many issues involving live soldiers to help with dead ones.

For Kineton, being kept up all night by the same battle was obviously getting a bit of a pain. Nobody was going to help them, so Kineton's residents clearly had to sort it out for themselves.

But how do you get rid of two armies of ghosts? Kill another army and send it out to drive them away?

No. The solution was far simpler. Aware that many battlefield corpses still lay scattered around Edgehill, the villagers reasoned that if they gave all these poor slain soldiers a Christian burial, the apparitions would cease. They were right. Three months after Parliament fired the first shots, the battlefield finally fell silent.

***

So why was I here tonight? All of that finished in 1643. I was more than 360 years late. But maybe not. In the 1860s, over 200 years after the battle, the ghosts were suddenly at it again, the battle clearly visible and witnessed by many from the ridge of Edge Hill. Something had stirred them only momentarily, for once their re-enactment was over they vanished and haven't been seen since.

But their battle is still *heard*. To this day, it is common local knowledge that every so often, on cold, dark nights, the crash and thunder of battle reverberates around the forbidding surrounding hills.

And it was the outline of those distant hills that I stared at now; dark clouds scudding across the top of the blackened Edge Hill ridge against a moonlit sky. Parked beside the battle monument in this shadowy, empty country lane, I sat sipping tea and wondering about my sanity. It was ten o'clock. My mind flicked to the warmth of my sofa, and to the warm glow of the fireplace. What on earth was I doing here, sitting in a car, listening out for the sounds of a battle that finished centuries ago?

At first, I have to admit, I was more concerned about the footing hazards at this particular spot than the risk of anything actually happening. I had the strong feeling that any attempt to leave the car would again render me a mud-splattered wreck. But then my overactive imagination started hassling me. What if something did happen? What if the lane ahead suddenly became filled with the ghosts of long-dead Royalist infantrymen? What if butchered Roundhead horsemen came galloping down the road towards me? I glanced nervously at the dark silhouette of the monument before me, in size and shape looking more like a gravestone than I'd remembered it. OK, keep calm, I thought. Just another four hours and then I'll be off.

Four hours? Four long, dark hours? But I had to stay. When the sounds of battle are heard here, it tends to nearly always be either on anniversary night, or during the week preceding Christmas. So if I didn't hear anything tonight, I'd be spending every night for a week up here in December. In the light of that, I had to seriously hope that I would indeed be approached by a group of dead soldiers.

Shivering at the thought I pulled away onto the lane, this time without feeling any need to head-butt the steering wheel, and headed for the Castle Inn. I was neglecting my post, but traditionally nothing much seems to happen before midnight anyway. And half a pint of Adnams Southwold would bolster me considerably if needing to deal with any phantom horseman later in the night. Five pints of Old Hooky, of course, and I'd be joyriding their horses, slapping their helmets and telling them they were my best mates. But I was driving, so ploughing headlong into them would have been the more likely scenario. 'Sorry, officer. I know this sounds silly but, due to a sudden fear of ghosts, I drank five pints of strong beer, and then crashed into this monument to avoid a Parliamentarian pikeman in the middle of the road. You've got to laugh, haven't you?'

So Adnams it would be. An interesting lot, Adnams. They are fantastically old, older than the Castle Inn and older than the Civil War. In fact, the first records of beer production on their current site go back to a time when even the Battle of Agincourt lay seventy years in the future, the Mongol Golden Horde were rampaging along the coast of the Black Sea, and everybody thought the world was flat. Incredible. Even more incredible is that Adnams don't seem bothered. Accessing their website, you struggle to find anything much about their origins at all. The site is a tribute to modern-thinking political correctness – churning out corporate clichés and banging on about carbon footprints and community, but seeming to forget all about that wonderfully long history. Only when you look carefully and delve deeper do you find mention of it, amazingly accompanied by a disclaimer: 'Adnams today is looking to the future rather than the past . . . '

Hmm, perhaps it's the reason for their 1345 entry

in the record books that bothers them so much: 'Johanna de Corby and 17 other "ale wives" of Southwold were charged by the manorial court with breaking the assize of ale.'

So, they, or their predecessors at the brewery, were up before the judge in 1345. Are they still feeling a bit edgy? Not on our account, I hope. As it was almost 700 years ago, I think we can let it go now, can't we?

I walked into the warmth of an almost empty lounge bar. The landlady eyed me suspiciously. I think she half-recognised me, but probably couldn't quite equate me with the filthy tramp who'd accompanied the loud, jovial, fat man a few days earlier.

On the bar was a booklet I hadn't seen during my earlier visit. If I'd wanted some light reading to settle my nerves a little, then this was surely not it. 'The Ghosts of Edgehill' proved to be interesting if not entirely intelligent reading given my circumstances.

The first few pages covered much of what I knew already; of the recurring ghostly battles and the spectral invasion of Kineton. It also told of 'Prince Rupert's anniversary gallop on a white charger across the hill'.

I glanced edgily through the inn's small window at the branches of a leafless tree blowing in the wind, and imagined the dark hill and battlefield beyond. The bar door suddenly opened behind me and I jumped out of my skin, spilling beer into my lap.

What was it with this place? Why couldn't I just come here and be normal? On my first visit I'd manifested into a mud-caked mess, and now I'd be remembered as the 'half-pint late-night loner who pissed himself'. I decided to stay in my seat until my jeans dried out naturally – vigorous rubbing wouldn't have improved my image at all.

The couple who'd alarmed me so terribly by having the audacity to open a pub door nodded politely to me as they passed my table, blissfully unaware of the trouble they'd caused my trousers.

More time to read, anyway. The booklet went on to debate the Prince Rupert apparition. Local stories also connect this ghostly horseman with a Captain Kingsmill. This seemed more likely to me. Not that I'm suddenly an expert on those most likely to haunt. It's just that if there's one thing that seems fairly consistent in ghost stories, it's the tendency of the supposed haunter to have died in the place they're haunting. I could therefore see no reason for Prince Rupert to have come back here years later to haunt a place where he'd not only not died, but seems by many accounts to have had a thoroughly good time.

Sir Henry Kingsmill, on the other hand, didn't have a good time at Edgehill. He might have been *having* a good time, but it would almost certainly have been ruined by the cannonball that hit him. You tend not to get back up after something like that, and two monuments to Captain Kingsmill can be found in Radway Church, one a normal monumental slab, the other an impressive effigy. Now, the chances of him being the man on the white charger are much greater, I think.

To me, it didn't really matter who it was, just that he was reputed to be out there on anniversary night, tonight, and I was soon to be out there too. By 1 a.m. it'd probably be just the two of us. I only hoped he didn't feel like socialising.

I read on. Radway offered more ghosts. 'A pair of legs clad in white stockings and buckled shoes seen to disappear upstairs in the house where King Charles is supposed to have had breakfast after the battle in Radway village', and the very strange 'cottage where blood drops through the ceiling to the floor beneath, an experience said to be shared by most of its owners'.

There was also mention of Sir Edmund Verney (he whose hand was removed while refusing to relinquish the standard). The story of Sir Edmund didn't end with his valiant defiance and subsequent murder, or even with his participation in ghostly re-enactments. After his severed hand had been removed from the Royal Standard, it was returned to his home, Claydon House in Buckinghamshire, with full honours. And here the story becomes rather confusing. The pamphlet claimed that Sir Edmund still haunted Edgehill, a handless spectre roaming the battlefield in search of his missing hand. And yet I'd previously heard he now haunts Claydon House, rather than Edgehill. His ghost is well known at his old home. Again handless, the phantom searches the house, rather than the battlefield, for the missing hand. The theory is that when the Royalists returned his grisly mitt to its rightful home, his ghost came along too. The apparition usually appears at the bottom of staircase, probably having grabbed the banister at the top, suddenly realising he had nothing to grab it *with*, and descending rapidly to the bottom – but that's just my theory. So is Sir Edmund commuting between both sites, or are they two different ghosts?

Another version of the Claydon House haunting makes more sense – that the hand itself haunts the house, knocking on bedroom doors in the dead of night. So . . . the handless Sir Edmund is at Edgehill, and the *hand* is at Claydon. That's better. Perfectly feasible now.

For me personally, the pamphlet's most worrying report concerned 'travellers being jostled as if in a crowd and seeing faces of long-dead soldiers'. This one bothered me. I eyed the door to the car park, wondering if a quick sprint to the car might take me past any dead soldiers before they could jostle me.

My mind made up, I polished off my half and strode boldly towards the door. As I did so, I couldn't help but notice the landlady's horrified expression. She was staring, mouth open, at my beer-soaked crotch.

The Castle Inn, Edgehill, may well have been the place that King Charles I raised his standard, but there is no doubt that it is where I dropped mine.

I made it to the car at a trot and headed back down the gloomy lanes. I decided to terrify myself straight away by parking up at Radway Church. If Captain Kingsmill was about tonight, then here could be a good place to find him. I sat staring wide-eyed at gravestones for a short while and then resumed my journey, driving slowly around the outer circuit of the battlefield, window open so as not to miss any sudden volleys of cannon fire.

Every shadow looked ominous out here, every hedge forbidding, every distant tree took on its own frightening persona.

Of course, if I'd really wanted to see some military action tonight – really wanted to be jostled by soldiers – I could have just driven down one of the lanes that cut straight across the middle of the battlefield. These lanes are now Ministry of Defence property and strictly off limits. I'm sure a strange car with a jittery driver approaching a secure MOD compound at 1 a.m. would have stirred a few sleeping soldiers into action, if not dead ones. The venture could also have got me killed, hit by an RPG just to be on the safe side, so I decided to keep circling the outer edges.

And this I did until nearly 3 a.m. Nothing. Not a musket fired in anger. I ended the night where I'd started it, parked up at the Civil War monument. I stepped out of my car and peered through the hedge at the inky black, silent fields beyond. A sudden gust of cold wind caught me full on, almost taking me off my feet. Shuddering, I walked back to the car.

As I settled in my seat I stared at the treetops and hedges. They were still. The wind had dropped completely; indeed, I couldn't recall a breeze of any note for the last hour or two. The icy blast that hit me had been a freak gust, completely out of the blue. As I drove the empty lanes towards Banbury and the motorway home, I wondered whether I really had been hit by a gust of wind.

Or had I been jostled?

The Battle of Chalgrove and the Charge of the Duck Brigade

In which the intrepid Pillock contributes to the Mission greatly, by listening to ducks and bunny-hopping sideways into a stream

lways go to the pub. Remember that.

With Pete's sound advice still ringing in my ears, I arrived in Chalgrove, Oxfordshire, on a sunny November lunchtime. Pete's advice sounded so clearly in my mind because Pete was sitting next to me, repeating it over and over again, determined to ensure I avoid a repetition of what had become known as the 'Edgehill error'. And, of course, determined to get to the pub. With only one battlefield done, this man's ability to browbeat and irritate had already severely tested my resolve to stick with the Mission and now he was off again, though I realised I'd be a fool not to listen a second time.

But the Crown in Chalgrove, despite the Royalist connotations of its name, was to be no Castle Inn. In fact it would prove of absolutely no help whatsoever. Unless the kind of help you were looking for had nothing to do with the English Civil War, which I'm quite sure most patrons wouldn't have been looking for in any case. I think, in fact, that if any type of survey were ever carried out on the subject, only a tiny percentage of UK pub customers would say that their primary reason for visiting public houses was for matters relating to the English Civil War. A very tiny percentage.

We stepped into the lounge bar, a moderately pleasant carpeted L-shaped room, and were immediately struck by . . . nothing. Apart from a large mirror over the fireplace and a few tables, the room was noticeable for its amazing lack of anything. No paintings, no ornaments, candles, customers, bar staff. Just nothing. In abundance.

And then I spotted it.

A brass plaque among the nothingness, attached to a black upright beam. A gleaming brass commemorative plaque. I marched up to it, fully expecting to see my first Battle of Chalgrove memorabilia. The plaque read:

IN 1832 ON THIS SPOT,
NOTHING HAPPENED.

Brilliant. I glanced around the quiet empty room,

chuckled and followed Pete through to the public bar.

The public bar was another story altogether. It was horrible. Almost tripping over a freestanding twin-bar electric fire, plonked unceremoniously right in the middle of the big, bright, tile-floored room, I stared aghast at the state of the place. I'm a bit fussy with pubs, I have to admit. I prefer a pub to look like a pub. This room looked more like an old-style BR station café, or possibly a dilapidated launderette. No attempt whatsoever had been made to give the room any atmosphere at all, never mind a pleasant one.

The walls were covered in patches of roughly plastered repairs, while a few advertising posters and two white marker boards provided the room's only decor. Each whiteboard featured crudely drawn pictures of smoking spliffs, along with captions, one explaining that you smell and the other suggesting you skin-up. A pool table and wall-mounted jukebox completed the picture.

One of the pub's four customers, an elderly man in a flat cap, got up from his seat, glared politely at us and paced into the gents' toilets clutching his pint to his chest and swinging a suspicious-looking carrier bag. Two young girls sat happily discussing hair-dyes at the bar, while alongside them at a nearby table, a middle-aged woman, glammed-up as if it were Saturday night at Stringfellows, sipped her wine and gave me a hugely elaborate wink.

'Seems nice in here,' beamed Pete happily, as he stepped up to the bar to study the beers on offer. 'What you having? You can have any bitter you like as long as it's Morland Original.'

In all truth, once the jukebox started playing and Pete racked up the pool balls, the pub's atmosphere grew on me and took on a charm all of its own. Not so much the atmosphere of a pub, but more that of a '50s and '60s-style café – the sort you see on *Heartbeat* and the like. The bar staff and customers around the bar were friendly and smiley. And once our pool game reached its climax, not only friendly and smiley, but friendly, smiley and stunned. Totally stunned.

You see, as far as I'm aware, Pete's version of pool is quite different from versions played elsewhere in the world. He calls it 'Devon Rules United States Air Force Pool' and it seems to have come about through a confusion of two kinds of pool he played as a teenager. One was typical US pool he'd learned as a civilian employee on a USAF base, and played over huge areas of the world. The other was Devon Rules Pool, which seems to have only been played in a tiny Devon village by Pete and twenty confused locals.

The one outstandingly different aspect of Devon Rules Pool is that, whereas in most pool games you pot the black ball in the pocket of your choice to finish the game, in Devon Rules Pool you nominate the pocket in which you intend to pot the black before you start the game. This pre-game nomination works fine, but it has one major flaw for the players involved, and that is that nobody else in the entire world is aware of it. And so, when a Devon Rules Pool player plays in front of a pub full of people, he invariably ends up looking a complete idiot.

And so it was that, at the end of our first frame, I

found myself with the black ball hanging on the lip of a pocket and proceeded to do something apparently deranged. To the five people watching, it looked easy. A nice gentle tap-in would win me the game for sure. A nice gentle tap-in, almost impossible to miss. But as a Devon Rules Pool player I had other things on my mind. The ball in question wasn't hanging over *my* pocket. My agenda was to keep the black ball out of that pocket.

I stepped up to the table, gritted my teeth and grunted with sheer effort as I smacked a simple tap-in at 150mph, striking the ball so ferociously that the balls shot from the very pool table, the black ball flying high into the air and almost reaching the bar. My cheeks coloured as I paced across the room to retrieve it, the wide-mouthed faces of all around me registering total astonishment. To them, my shot had been psychotic, wild, totally inexplicable. Collecting my ball I came up face to face with Glam-woman. She winked a slow wink at me, and ... oh no ... surely not ... her tongue darted out, seductively moistening her bright-red lips. I smiled, mumbled something about having maybe overhit my last shot, and backed away from the bar.

'You're in there,' muttered Pete, re-racking the pool table. 'I had my eyes on that one, you jammy little sod!'

I grimaced and glanced around the room. The two bar staff were whispering and chuckling, probably discussing my antics, the two girls at the bar were now moving into advanced hair colourings and highlightings, and the old man with the carrier bag was glaring straight at me, fingering his bag menacingly.

'Born To Run' struck up on the jukebox and I briefly considered the option, but there was work to be done here, and Pete just wasn't doing it today.

As he cued off behind me, I decided I should ask the bar staff about the total lack of Civil War memorabilia in the pub.

I walked up to the bar and asked the twenty-something barman exactly that.

'Civil War?' he replied, perplexed.

'Yeah, you know, the Battle of Chalgrove. I just wondered if anyone round here took any interest in it.'

The barman burst out laughing. 'The . . . Battle . . . of . . . Chalgrove?' he repeated slowly. His brow furrowed.

Glam-woman came to his rescue. 'Yeah, you daft little git. Didn't you know about the battle? Bloody kids nowadays! There's a monument to it out by the industrial estate.'

'Oh, is that what that thing is? I always wondered,' mumbled the barman.

Glam-woman redirected her attention to me. I knew about the monument already, and planned to head out there after the next game of pool, but her next piece of proffered info was quite heartening after three 'no Civil War interest whatsoever' pubs on the row.

'You seen the pub across the road? The Red Lion? You wanna go over there.'

She was right. I really did.

'They like all that war stuff in the Red Lion, they do,' she continued.

I was all ready to dive through the Red Lion's

doors, but Pete was now ordering a pint from the barman (whose lifetime of wondering about the mysterious monument on his doorstep was now over). It was back to more humiliation on the green baize. Pete potted virtually all his balls within three shots and then dutifully missed a succession of unmissable blacks.

The game went to the wire, and finished exactly as the first had done, with the black ball in orbit. As I retrieved it, Glam-woman smacked my backside, the old man glared at me and the bar staff laughed out loud. A young man, who'd just arrived, plonked himself at the bar and belched. It was time to go.

'How did it go?' the barman asked the new arrival.

New-arrival replied with a follow-up belch so loud that the walls seemed to vibrate. This answer seemed to satisfy everyone, and all at the bar nodded solemnly. Whatever 'it' was evidently hadn't gone well at all.

As I grabbed my coat and followed Pete to the door to the sound of a row breaking out over visible roots, the old man gave me a sudden and completely unexpected smile. I smiled back, almost tripping over the electric fire in surprise.

'Did you see that?' I asked Pete as we hit the cold November air. 'The old boy who glared at us for half an hour just smiled at me!'

Pete considered this for a moment. 'Probably just wind,' he decided, and jumped into the car.

This was a bonus. I'd fully intended to let him loose in the Red Lion before driving the short distance to the battlefield, but I wasn't about to look a gift horse in the mouth, and set off down the road to the fields surrounding Monument Industrial Park. En route we discussed the Crown, or rather argued bitterly over it. Our tastes in pubs are somewhat different, and while I thought the Crown public bar looked a bit of a mess, Pete quite rightly pointed out that the Crown is a 'real pub': unpretentious, friendly, and caring more about making people feel welcome and at home than about putting on airs and graces. He also pointed out that I was a twat. It was obviously something he felt strongly about.

The monument itself is much bigger and grander than the small roadside stone at Edgehill. But although it stands on the battlefield of Chalgrove, it's not actually there to commemorate the Battle of Chalgrove itself, but rather a man who was mortally wounded during the battle. The monument was erected in 1843, exactly two hundred years after the event, and dedicated to John Hampden, he who, as mentioned earlier, held a strong dislike for giving Charles money. John Hampden was the reason that the Battle of Chalgrove stands out from the multitude of other 'smaller' battles in Civil War history. He was such a high-profile Parliamentarian that his death came as a major blow and shock to Parliament.

And for that reason, and that alone, I'd chosen the battlefield at Chalgrove to visit ahead of all the other sites of small battles, skirmishes and sieges that occurred during the extended gap between the war's first two major confrontations at Edgehill in October 1642 and Adwalton Moor in June 1643. Well, that and the fact it's only a 25-minute drive from home.

Not that the extended gap hadn't been action-packed. After Edgehill, militias and armed bands sprung up everywhere. Fights broke out up and down the land. England became a divided and dangerous country. But a huge clash of arms of the Edgehill variety, involving full-scale armies, had been missing. By mid-June 1643, both Charles's army and Essex's troops were back in close proximity to one another in Oxfordshire. Something nasty was bound to happen, and it happened at Chalgrove.

The monument stands close to the spot where things went horribly wrong for John Hampden. The battlefield spreads out all around it, a wide Oxfordshire plain stretching into the distance, but it was here, within yards of this monument, that on 18 June 1643 John Hampden was struck by two Royalist musket balls to the shoulder. Allegedly.

There is, to this day, debate on exactly how Hampden was wounded, but wounded he was. And the day wasn't just a bit of a disaster for him. It was without doubt a day the Parliamentarians would rather just hadn't happened at all.

Our old friend Prince Rupert was the Royalist leader on the day. He'd obtained information from an enemy deserter that a Parliamentarian pay wagon was in the area. At Edgehill, Rupert and his men had galloped on from the battlefield in order to enjoy a spot of looting, and so they weren't about to let an opportunity like a lorry-load of money pass them by.

On 17 June, pushing his uneaten evening meal aside (probably), he led a force of 1,100 cavalry, 500 infantry and 400 dragoons from the King's headquarters at Oxford.

Travelling through the night, he arrived in the

Oxfordshire village of Chinnor during the early hours of the morning and came across a 200-strong force of Parliamentarian dragoons. It's not recorded as to whether these dragoons were eating breakfast at the time, but if they were they'd picked the wrong Royalist general to mess with. He killed fifty of them and captured a hundred and twenty.

But there was no pay wagon. This early-morning skirmish gave Rupert's game away, and the pay wagon fled the area. His plan foiled, and another meal completely ruined, the Prince headed back towards Oxford. And he might have made it had word of his whereabouts not reached Colonel John Hampden and his Green Coat cavalry at the nearby village of Watlington. Hampden saw the opportunity to cut Rupert off from Oxford and, sending an urgent request for the Earl of Essex to cut off Rupert's retreat at a local river, he galloped out in pursuit of the Cavaliers.

Hampden's only problem on the day was that he caught them.

On the very fields where Pete and I now stood, Rupert turned to face his pursuers. And what exactly Pete was doing by the side of these fields at this moment suddenly became of concern to me. I'd assumed his bizarre hopping, hand-clapping dance had something to do with the cold north wind blowing across the unprotected plains. But if it was some ancient rain dance, then it was certainly effective, for within seconds the previously sunny afternoon gave way to a sudden and vicious downpour. Running for the car, Pete gave a loud whooping yell, possibly due to the icy drops drenching us to the skin, possibly in anticipation of an enforced early pub break, or maybe as a climax to his tribal rain-making.

I was looking forward to the Red Lion. Any woman who deemed my backside worth slapping could hardly be relied upon, but Glam-woman had said this was a 'Civil War pub' and my expectations were high.

But first we had to get in there. The tiny bridged stream running across the front of its roadside front garden wasn't exactly of moat-like proportions and certainly didn't present much of a barrier, but the massed ranks of ducks that suddenly spilled over its banks and charged us World War One style did. The moment we stepped from the car, they were everywhere. I watched in astonishment as they completely surrounded the car, actually stepping on our feet as they busily marched to and fro.

If Pete's rain dance had been a slightly disturbing sight to behold, it has to be said that his duck-trot disappeared over the other side of ridiculous. I watched in sheer delight as a seventeen-stone man hopped ballet-style through hordes of quacking ducks, swayed dangerously for a moment and then, inexplicably, tried to jump the stream.

He later said he'd been put off balance by the ducks, and that a jump represented a better option than a fall. Whatever brought the decision on, it was a bad one. He covered no ground at all. It was just a sideways two-feet hop, followed by a drop and a splash. At the very moment of execution, the old man from the Crown, he of the sunny disposition, appeared from the door of the Red Lion.

His face summed it up for me. Half an hour earlier he'd watched these two clowns failing miserably to pot a succession of the easiest pool shots he'd ever seen, and now here they were again, one of them engulfed in ducks, the other bunny-hopping sideways into a stream. He simply grimaced, shook his head, pulled his cap down sharply and marched off up the road, carrier bag swaying in the breeze.

I was helpless, almost crying with laughter. It was difficult to say which of us looked the least dangerous proposition; the one howling with demented mirth among a sea of ducks in an empty street, or the one standing in the stream.

We finally walked through the Red Lion door. Well, I walked – Pete slopped – into a delightful little beamed-ceiling pub with an inglenook fireplace and a warren-like layout of tables tucked away into every cosy, private corner. And better even than its warm and friendly layout was its promised array of memorabilia. Above the fireplace hung two sketches depicting a Civil War siege at nearby Wallingford. Beyond a partitioning half-wall hung two info-prints, one entitled 'The Battle of Chalgrove Field', the other all about John Hampden. There was also a small portrait of John Hampden.

Pete waded to the bar and ordered himself a pint, and me the detested but obligatory Diet Coke. I sat down at a table and was further delighted to realise that the middle-aged couple at the table behind me were American tourists, who were busily discussing the battle. For the first time on my pub visits thus far, someone else was present for the same reason I was. Unless you count

Pete, but I don't. The famous old seaside hat proclaiming the legend 'ONLY HERE FOR THE BEER' would have been embarrassingly accurate headgear for him during any one of our battlefield visits.

I eavesdropped intently on their conversation. Either the American man was winding the American woman up or he didn't have the faintest idea what had happened at Chalgrove and was too proud to admit it:

'So whose side were we on?'

'Nobody's side, Delores. We weren't in this war. Not officially. Not until the end.'

'Whose side were we on at the end?'

'Nobody's side, Delores. We just came to pick up the pieces.'

WHAT? Pick up the pieces? An American peace-keeping force in the 1640s? An American anything-force??

'So who was fighting here, honey?'

'The Brits.'

'Who were the Brits fighting?'

'A mixture. Total mixture. Normanders, Vikings, Hollanders, French.'

'Who won?'

'WHO WON? The Brits, of course. This is still Britain right here, ain't it?!'

I was hearing it, but I couldn't believe it. Was he serious? Was he trying desperately to keep a straight face? Unprompted, he offered a little more priceless information.

'Country used to be a total mixture. The Brits drove the Normanders and everyone else out. Got their country back.'

'Wow. To think that all happened here.'

'Here and all over Britain, Delores. They just drove them back into Europe.'

He began chuckling. I thought this was going to be his cue to admit he was taking the piss.

But no. The chuckle was followed by a loud, conspiratorial whisper.

'With . . . just a little help from us [chuckle].'

'I thought you said we weren't over here, honey?'

'Oh, we get around [another chuckle]. What our boys do officially and what they really do . . . that's two different things. Brits have never taken on Europe without us anytime, have they?'

Pete arrived back at the table and mercifully drowned out their conversation with a series of clonks, splashes and glass chinks. I sat in mild disbelief, pondering the concept of an enduringly pure British separatist race who drove the Normans and the Vikings out six hundred years after they'd arrived. And the Hollanders too. Not to mention the French.

How clever of them to have done the whole thing under the cover of the English Civil War.

Nobody suspected a thing.

Having given Pete plenty of time to bolster his alcoholic defences, I finally suggested we get back outside for a further spot of battlefield-staring. Pete registered his usual acceptance with a few bitter four-letter profanities and we stepped outside into the kingdom of the ducks.

I glanced back at the Red Lion as we reached the car. For the first time since the Castle Inn, I'd been pleasantly surprised. Pulling away through a blanket (or duvet) of flapping, quacking ducks, we headed back to the battlefield where, back in 1643, the surprise Rupert had planned for the Parliamentarians had been anything but pleasant.

For when Rupert turned to face his pursuers, he'd done so with a degree of cunning and reserve you probably wouldn't have expected from one so gung-ho and cavalier as he. He hid his troops behind hedges and undergrowth in an attempt to ambush the oncoming enemy, rather than deploy the usual Rupert tactic of charging headlong into the opposition.

The oncoming enemy, unfortunately, saw him at it, decided it looked like a very cunning idea indeed, and hid behind hedges of their own with a view to firing muskets at him. However, they did this in full view of Rupert. Now, having a six-year-old daughter, I know a little of the dynamics of hide and seek, and it just doesn't work properly if you both hide at once and both know where each other are. Rupert obviously realised this because, throwing cunning plans out the window and reverting to type, he charged straight at the Parliamentarian hedges.

The panic the Parliamentarian's must have felt as Rupert's cavalry came bounding through their cover was enough to totally disorganise them. Worse still, Rupert sent another regiment around the side of the hedges.

As Royalists ploughed into the panicking defences from all directions, it became quickly clear this wasn't going to end in any Edgehill-style stalemate. This was fast turning into a slaughter.

The Parliamentarians broke and ran, fleeing for their lives.

But the unflappable John Hampden met them as they fled towards him, reorganising the retreating rabble into a fighting force and somehow encouraging them to charge back across the field at the Royalist positions. It was a brave counterattack, but it ended in tears. Charging first through musket fire and then into a ferocious Royalist reception, the Parliamentarians were utterly routed. Worse still, Hampden himself received his mortal injury during the charge, and was carried from the field by his retreating troops.

The enemy at his rear defeated, Rupert resumed his journey to Oxford. But what of the enemy ahead of him? John Hampden had had the foresight to alert Essex and make sure he was there to head Rupert off. This being Essex, of course, Prince Rupert and his troops crossed the river and made it back to the safety of Oxford unhindered. It wasn't that Essex hadn't tried – he was just late.

The day had been a terrible one for Parliament. Percentage-wise, their casualties were horrific. They'd lost a capable commander and a fine politician, and despite all of their efforts, Rupert had returned to base with only twelve men less than he'd set out with.

The wounded John Hampden was carried to the nearby town of Thame, where he lay dying for six agonising days in a house in the high street. Such was the stature of Hampden that King Charles offered to send his own physician to Thame to treat him. Or, just possibly, to ask if he'd reconsider the loan applications.

Hampden died there in the high street on 24 June 1643, but almost two hundred years later the story of his day at Chalgrove, and also his body, would resurface.

This was thanks largely to a man named George Grenville, Lord Nugent. The story of Hampden's death had remained a talking point throughout the intervening centuries, and confusion reigned as to just how he'd actually received the wounds that killed him. The most common report was that, as mentioned earlier, he was hit in the shoulder by musket fire. The alternative version was that his own pistol had exploded in his hand, causing him terrible injuries.

This uncertainty proved too much for Lord Nugent. In 1828, he obtained permission to open John Hampden's coffin and find out for sure. Hampden had been buried in the chancel of Great Hampden church, Buckinghamshire, which in 1828 was having its floor relaid. The building work provided Lord Nugent with an excellent window of opportunity, and he and a team of friends, servants and grave-diggers converged on Great Hampden church to exhume John Hampden's body.

They immediately ran into a serious problem. They had no idea which coffin beneath the chancel floor belonged to John Hampden. Some had nameplates or initials, and so could be discounted, but none could be found bearing the name John Hampden.

The party eventually settled on a coffin with a badly corroded and unreadable nameplate as being the most likely. Some of those present disagreed, feeling that the coffin looked to have been from an era predating Hampden. When opened it was found to be filled with sawdust and, judging by a written account of the exhumation, this must have had quite a preservative effect on the body within. The face was of firm white flesh with blood vessels still visible, eyes filmed over, teeth in good condition. There was a brown moustache and light stubble upon the chin, and brown hair, tied at the top, hung down seven or eight inches. The account continues:

> . . . he was five feet nine inches in height, apparently of great muscular strength, of a vigorous and robust frame; forehead broad and high; the skull altogether well formed, such a one as the imagination could conceive capable of great exploits.

Nugent, who strongly favoured the musket-shot theory, examined the shoulders himself. No gunshot wounds could be found. An examination of the hands was carried out by Nugent's friend William James Smith, who records:

> When I took up the right hand it was contained in a sort of funeral glove like a pocket. On raising it I found it was entirely detached from the arm: the bones of the wrist and hand were much displaced, and had evidently been splintered by some violent concussion, only the ends of the fingers were held together by the ligaments. The two bones of the fore-arm for about three inches

above the wrist were without flesh or skin, but there were no marks of amputation. The left hand was in a similar glove, but it was firmly attached to the arm, and remained so when the glove was drawn away. There were slight portions of flesh upon the hand; the bones were complete, and still held in their places by the ligaments which supported them.

At this point it would seem that the evidence was fairly conclusive, especially as a servant at Great Hampden House, who had been present at the exhumation, returned to the house and recognised a portrait of John Hampden, painted in 1640, as being the face in the coffin.

But then things become confused. In later years Nugent wrote to a friend, stating that he didn't believe the 'skeleton' that he'd studied had been that of John Hampden, but of somebody, either a lady or gentleman, who had died quietly in their bed.

Which is rather different from Smith's account! According to Smith's description, there shouldn't have been any confusion over the corpse's gender. Was Nugent so keen to prove his own theory correct that he deliberately distorted facts? Or had Smith's account been false?

When we reached the 1843 memorial beside Chalgrove Field again, it proved as inconclusive as the rest of the tale. An inscription, written by Lord Nugent himself, states only that Hampden 'received a wound from which he died'. And so the mystery surrounding John Hampden's death remains.

Taking one last, lingering look at the empty hedge-lined flat where so many Parliamentarians lost their lives, we climbed into the car and drove back to the village, noting on arrival that the ducks had now fanned out to block the entire road. Driving at a snail's pace through the anatine throng, Pete wound down his window and stared intently into the middle distance.

'What are you looking at?' I reluctantly enquired.

'I'm not looking at anything. I'm listening.'

'Listening to what?'

'The ducks.'

Listening to the ducks? Maybe he felt that having now spent a short period of his life in a stream, he'd be able to understand them. A sort of Tarzan-like figure, who'd very briefly shared the hardship of a duck's life in the streams of England. Tarzan of the ducks.

'Why are you listening to the ducks?'

'I'm trying to hear an echo.'

'An echo of what?'

'Ducks.'

'What?'

'I'm trying to hear a duck echo.'

Oh, of course. That was fine then.

'Why would you want to hear a duck echoing?'

'Ah, because they don't, you see.'

'They don't what?'

'Echo. Ducks don't echo. It's a fact. Ducks have no echo!'

I felt that the American story of the British Civil War against ancient European colonists had been enough claptrap for one day, but here was Pete opening a brand-new front in the war on common sense.

I offered as dignified a response as I could muster. 'Bollocks!'

'No, they really don't. Look it up.'

I resolved to do precisely the opposite and pursued the matter no further. Pete wound the window up, looking extremely self-satisfied. There'd obviously been no duck-echo today, at least.

We pulled into the Lamb's car park. The Lamb is a lovely thatched-cottage building on the outskirts of Chalgrove. It's divided into two rooms, one a games area and the other a big, refurbished, pleasant, family-eating room – pleasant because refurbishment hadn't stripped it of its charms, and had allowed it to retain that 'olde worlde' look. The walls were adorned with an abundance of Victorian-style adverts and prints, along with a fair number of stuffed fish and animals (something for any chance visitors from Kineton to enjoy).

The beer on offer was limited, Greene King's Abbot being the only real ale available. Pete wasn't bothered. Ducks don't echo – all was right with his world. And in any case, if only one beer's around, you'd want it to be a beer like Abbot Ale, one of my favourites and hailing from Bury St Edmunds – a town recording beer production at a date predating even Adnams by over two centuries. Unlike Adnams, Greene King are very proud of this great age, even if the beer brewed back then wasn't on their current site. They pretty much lay claim to it anyway – the very name Abbot Ale alludes to the fact that in 1086, only twenty years after William the Conqueror's

Norman invasion, the Domesday Book notes that the town's *cerevisiarii*, or ale brewers, were servants of the Abbot of the Great Abbey of St Edmundsbury.

Oblivious to its history and not giving a toss anyway, Pete stormed into his beer and blathered on about our visit so far to anybody who'd listen, complaining particularly bitterly about his time in the stream and gaining huge sympathy from an elderly couple at a nearby table. I carried out my standard Civil War memorabilia check and came up with another blank. Two out of three blanks at Edgehill, and the same at Chalgrove.

Realising I'd had nothing but a bag of crisps since the previous evening, I studied the menu, and immediately noted the presence of grilled swordfish. This was only of interest to me because the same dish had been on offer in the Red Lion. Is that normal? Two pubs in a small village about as far from the sea as you can get in England, both offering swordfish. Maybe there's more to that little stream than meets the eye. Three bags of crisps suddenly hurtled through the air from the general direction of Pete's seat at the bar, two smacking me in the face and one sailing over my head. Dinner had arrived before I'd even ordered.

While the walls of this pub offered nothing 'Civil War', I was in for a surprise from two old boys at the bar. Both had been animatedly discussing the merits of Oxford United Football Club since we'd arrived, and seemed to have come to the conclusion that there weren't any. It was at this point that one of them overheard Pete's ramblings and turned his attentions to the Battle of Chalgrove, just diverting Pete in time, who was moving on to ducks. Pete exchanged a few pleasantries with them and pulled his stool to theirs. I sat down at an adjacent table and listened.

The man was an absolute mine of information. He talked for maybe fifteen minutes, providing a rich seam of interesting little snippets on minor skirmishes that had taken place in surrounding villages. But by far the most fascinating titbit, to me at least, was the 'silent zone' on Chalgrove Field. This was the first time I had heard about the dead zone that I described in my introduction. An area of the battlefield where no animal will walk and over which no bird will fly. Initially, I thought maybe we were heading for another helping of Normander/duck echoes, but soon his colleague was joining in. I began scribbling notes.

This was something I had to find out more about.

It was at this point that I realised there was a man under my table.

I'd had no idea he was there. I just looked down, and saw a face looking up at me. To say I jumped is an understatement. Something akin to 'ARGHHWHAT!' involuntarily exploded from my wide-open mouth, and then everybody at the bar jumped too.

I looked down at the man in horror. The man looked up at me in horror. Suddenly he backed out, got to his feet and walked hurriedly to the door. I watched him leave, totally aghast. The four men at the bar stared at me for a moment and then casually resumed their conversation. I listened for a few moments more, but in a sense of wonder. Had I just imagined that? Why had nobody reacted?

'Er, excuse me,' I interrupted. 'What was that about? Any idea?'

'He likes legs,' answered the main talker, and with that the matter was closed.

Pete muffled a laugh, and then war talk resumed. For about the first time in my life, I wanted the conversation to be about something other than the English Civil War. Today was an odd one.

Struggling to reduce my heartbeat to safe levels, I relocated my pen and resumed note-taking. Pete was getting all the details I needed, not only asking if they knew 'why the phenomenon occurred', but also whether they knew of any 'agricultural chemicals that might possibly be to blame'. All of which was pretty sharp for somebody on their fifth pint of beer on a weekday lunchtime. In fact, Pete seemed to get sharper by the pint that day. He seemed to be in rewind, as if he'd started out drunk and got more sober with every beer he consumed. Look at the evidence – on five pints he was acting like some switched-on investigative journalist, on three pints he'd been listening to ducks, on two he'd jumped into a stream, and before his first he'd called the public bar at the Crown 'nice'.

My theory was blown apart the moment we stepped from the Lamb's door twenty minutes later. He'd had six pints and so should have, by my reckoning, been bordering on a professorship. Instead he sang 'You Are My Sunshine' to a passing dog and tried to get in the wrong car. As I sat tapping my fingers on the wheel of the correct car, watching my companion stumble around the car park in a state of 'Oh no, the bastard's driven off without me . . .

again' panic, I noticed a rather odd thing – a fifty-foot driveway, which led from the Lamb car park and terminated abruptly in front of a high fence. At the start of this seemingly useless piece of road stood a signpost requesting that you 'Drive Slowly'. The question had to be asked, why drive at all? Surely all that could be offered here was a two-second joyride straight into a fence.

My ponderings were interrupted by a fat drunkard falling into my car and swearing at me. I told him to put his seat belt on, and we set off for High Wycombe. There was no time to check out Chalgrove's dead zone today, but I resolved to do so at a later date. My calendar, for once, was full. At the weekend we were heading up to Yorkshire, to the battlefield of Adwalton Moor and, I had to admit, I was deeply troubled by the fact that Pete would be accompanying me.

With all the evidence gained over years of this man's lunchtime drinking habits and hatred of long journeys, I was taking him on an eight-hour round trip and staying in a hotel room with him. A hotel room attached to a pub. Obviously, standing in damp, empty fields isn't the only grounds on which I should be sectioned.

During an interesting half-hour journey home, during which I was treated to Pete's entire snoring repertoire, a thought that had been niggling at the back of my mind all day escaped from that terrible place and pushed itself forward for consideration . . . why was there no 'proper' monument at Chalgrove?

They had a Hampden memorial, sure, but not an out-and-out Civil War monument. Why not? And, just as at Edgehill, why were the tourist signs only noticeable for their complete non-existence? These places were home to some of England's most stunning and terrible moments in history, and yet there was barely a nod of official recognition. I suddenly felt extremely angry, and resolved to write to somebody about it. I didn't care who – just as long as whoever it was felt the full weight of my wrath. The milkman was going to get one hell of a note in the morning.

I eventually poured Pete out of the car at the Prince of Wales, Little Kingshill, and went home to write up my notes in the peace and quiet that exists in my home before my wife and daughter get there. Once they're home, 'peace' and 'quiet' are words only useful to describe wherever they've just come from.

Midway through my keyboard tapping, I somehow found myself unable to prevent my fingers typing the words 'duck' and 'echo' into an Internet search engine. Expecting nothing more than the outside chance of a googlewhack, I ended up staring aghast at the sheer volume of received results.

Page after page claimed ducks had no echo, and page after page refuted the claims. There was a whole scientific debate raging out there. Claptrap, I'd called it. I sat back heavily in my chair, realising that there were some things I knew absolutely nothing about.

After a long, reflective pause, I tentatively tapped in the words 'US intervention – Normanders – Vikings – Hollanders', and then decided not to look at any of the forty-four websites offered.

Adwalton Moor – The Fight for Dave-Land

In which the Author meets a shed-eating dog and discovers the 'joys' of the Northern Club Scene

Waking Pete on a Saturday morning is something very much akin to an exhumation. Having tried the doorbell (not working), the knocker (much too quiet) and shouting through the letterbox as loudly as I felt appropriate in a quiet cul-de-sac at six in the morning (hoarse whisper), I decided I'd have to dig him out.

I pulled back the heavy grey slab, revealing a thick clay soil beneath. For a few moments I fumbled in the cloying dirt, until my fingers fell upon something sharp and metallic. Pulling the key free and sliding the loose patio stone back into place, I tried once more on the bell before slipping the key into the lock and stepping inside the tomb.

There was an eerie silence in the darkness of Pete's hallway. I flicked the lamp switch, but the bulb had gone. Actually gone. The lamp had no bulb in it. I tried the main light. Same problem.

Advancing slowly through the dark I made my way to the staircase. At the bottom of the stairs I called 'PETE!' No answering snores emanated from the rooms above. I climbed the stairs and reached for the landing light switch. No bulb. Was this some kind of cleverly planned ambush?

I tentatively turned a bedroom doorknob, pushed open the door and peered into the gloom within. Something stirred in the bed. There was a grunt and then silence.

"Pete . . . ' I whispered.

'Pete,' I tried again.

Nothing. I walked towards the bed. The breathing sounded ragged, strange.

'Pete?' Nothing.

I reached forward and shook the sleeping bulk. There was another grunt, but no movement. I pulled back the duvet, and recoiled in horror (I seem to recoil in horror quite often in Pete's company).

Stepping back with my hand over my mouth, I stared aghast at the wholly unexpected sight of a huge Alsatian dog. What was that doing there?

It was still sleeping, but its eyes started to flicker and its nose twitched. I backed gingerly towards the door, missing the opening and leaning back against the light switch. This would be the first one to have a bulb attached to it, wouldn't it? The room became suddenly bathed in brilliant light and, alarmingly, the dog's eyes sprang open. Then the dog sprang too, out of bed and straight at me, barking and snarling with undiluted rage. I almost fell sideways from the room in my haste to get out of the way, somehow managing to slam the door in the advancing dog's face. The barking increased in intensity, the door looking as if it could easily give way under a sudden onslaught of claws and teeth.

A bleary-eyed apparition ambled from the next bedroom along. At first glance, I'd have to say that the dog looked better.

'What's going on?' mumbled Pete, clearly not yet with it. 'Why's there a dog in that room?'

'What?' I replied, incredulous. 'You mean you don't know? Isn't it yours?'

We stared at each other in startled silence, the door banging repeatedly as the Alsatian threw its body against it in a furious effort to reach me.

But Pete's face was slowly changing. With awareness creeping back into the dark recesses of his befuddled mind, something was dawning on him.

'Ben!' he said, clicking his fingers.

'Ben?' I replied.

'Ben,' he repeated with increased confidence. 'Met him in the pub last night.'

Moments like this seem to come thick and fast in Pete's life. Animals have often featured. He was once head-butted unconscious by a goat in a village high street. The same goat then repeated the feat two weeks later, knocking him out in a café. It's a long story. He'd also been removed from a racecourse for making 'vile and threatening' remarks to a horse. Another long story, but the culmination of four weeks' work in the horse's stable and a misguided bet.

But this was a new one. He now claimed to have met a dog named Ben in a pub and, it would appear, put him up for the night.

'How do you know his name's Ben?' I asked, glancing at the buckling door.

'Eh? No . . . not the dog. The dog's owner. Ben's the dog's owner. He's coming to Yorkshire with us.'

'Ben?'

'No, Dave.'

'Who's Dave?'

'The dog.'

It was some time later that I found myself cruising up the M1 motorway, a snoring lunatic in my passenger seat and a huge Alsatian dog resting its slobbery head on my shoulder.

During twenty minutes of frantic dressing and packing, the crazy-man beside me had managed only a brief explanation.

We were taking the dog to Leeds. Apparently to stay with relatives, although this part was confused. As far as I understood, Dave was being transported to an old drinking friend of Pete's. Ben, the man who had given Pete the dog at some point during a heavy boozing session the previous evening, was the old drinking friend's brother. Pete knew Ben vaguely, but theirs' had been only a nodding acquaintance.

Until last night. Last night Pete and Ben had got talking. Pete had talked of his trip to Yorkshire, and Dave's ride was agreed. Pete was fairly sure he'd been given some fare money for this favour but if this was so, it now belonged to the pub. I tried to ignore the wet tongue in my ear, and pondered the coming battlefield.

The situation in the north of England during the opening year of the Civil War had been much the same as in the rest of the country, with marches, sieges and skirmishes taking place regularly. The North's first major battle took place on 30 June 1643 at Adwalton Moor, and the confrontation might never have amounted to more than another siege operation, but for some rotten weather and coincidental marching.

The Battle of Adwalton Moor came less than a couple of weeks after Chalgrove in the south, and was the first of two major battles that took place in Yorkshire. Parliament's main commander in the area was Lord Fairfax, garrisoned in Bradford. The Royalist army was entrusted to the Earl of Newcastle. From February to June 1643, Newcastle had been busy protecting Queen Henrietta Maria at York, and so hadn't been able to take the short trip down the road to take on the Parliamentarian army.

When the Queen finally got out of his hair and left York, he turned his attentions to Fairfax. With 10,000 troops, he set out for Bradford. Needing a base local to his objective, he stormed the nearby Howley Hall on 21 June.

His path to Bradford was now clear, but the skies were not. Appalling weather, and possibly an excellent Howley Hall wine cellar, caused him to delay his attack on Bradford by nine days. By which time, of course, Fairfax was well aware that one was coming.

Fairfax had taken the previous few days to assess his chances of holding Bradford against a huge Royalist attack, and decided he didn't have any. With only 4,000 men under his command, he knew he couldn't just sit and wait for Newcastle to attack him. He had to seize the initiative, create an advantage. He decide on a dawn raid on Howley Hall. It was an excellent idea. The element of surprise could just possibly outweigh the heavy numerical odds.

The weather finally cleared on 30 June and Fairfax immediately set his plan in motion. However, in getting the Parliamentarians out of bed that morning, Fairfax would seem to have encountered the same problems I'd had with Pete. The planned 4 a.m. march finally got under way at 8 a.m., by which time Newcastle had also noted the change in weather conditions and was on the move. There would be no dawn surprise attack. The real surprise came for *both* armies. As 10,000 Royalists marched towards Bradford and 4,000 Parliamentarians marched towards Howley Hall, they suddenly met on the same road. A serious fight was now inevitable.

I glanced at my roadmap. We were about an hour away from our destination. The battlefield lies in an area just south of modern-day Leeds and Bradford, and in all truth I wasn't holding out much hope of there being much to see. Maps indicated that the area is now fairly urban and just off a major motorway intersection. My one glimmer of hope lay in the fact that the 'crossed swords 1643' legend seemed to indicate that the battlefield lay on a patch of land that, although completely surrounded by roads, was still moorland.

A frantic howl and a slobbery kiss on the back of my neck brought me to my senses. I breathed a sigh of relief. It wasn't Pete.

In all truth, Dave the dog was proving to be a better travelling companion than Pete, and not merely from a romantic point of view. They both grunted, dribbled and slobbered, but at least the dog was conscious. Pete had passed out the moment we pulled out of his drive, and it was only now, two and a half hours later, that he finally stirred. He awoke for the second time that Saturday morning in much the same way as the first, registering total surprise at being in the company of a dog.

By the time we were leaning against the car, drinking tea at Trowell Services, a canine head poking excitedly through the window between us, Pete had pieced together a little more information. He was now fairly sure that Dave was going to be living in Leeds. He remembered Ben saying something along the lines of 'not being able to cope with him any more'. He also had a funny feeling that Dave had eaten Ben's shed, but as a shed seemed an unlikely sort of thing to eat, we decided to give Dave the benefit of the doubt.

Trowell Services had kindly placed huge bowls of dog biscuits and water at their door, and Dave hungrily demolished every scrap of food and drank like a fish . . . or a thirsty dog . . . or Pete. He then showed his deep gratitude for Trowell's kindness by crapping on their lawn. I don't think I've ever stared at a lump of faeces as long as I did that one.

'What do we do?' asked Pete eventually.

'*We* don't do anything. *You* pick it up and put it in that dog bin over there.'

'Me?'

'You.'

'Pick it up?'

'Yes.'

'What with?'

'I don't know.'

A further five minutes' staring ensued. Finally Pete bought a newspaper, scanned a few pages and then put it to the sword. What an awful end for the *Express*. In some homes an *Express* could expect to be thoroughly read from front to back and to linger for days in a magazine rack, before being committed to the noble cause of recycling. But not this one. No. Glanced at for thirty seconds by a totally uninterested man at the side of a motorway, wiped in shit and thrown in a bin.

Our journey continued with a miserable Pete receiving all of Dave's salivary attentions. We finally pulled into a pleasant suburban road on the outskirts of Leeds at 11 a.m. Dave bounded from the car to meet his new owner, also named Dave. Dave's wife Anita gave us tea and biscuits and insisted she put us up for the night. Dave barked his approval. I told Anita that we'd booked to stay at a local pub and that I'd have to phone to check their cancellation terms. This I did while Dave, Dave and Pete chatted and barked – an amusing scenario as Pete had never been able to understand Dave's strong Yorkshire accent – any more than he could the barking. The local pub admitted they couldn't give a toss whether we stayed or not, so Dave took in our bags and promised to show us the nightlife of Leeds. Human Dave, that is. And I think that's what he said.

We got back on the road at 11.30 a.m. and, fifteen minutes later, pulled off the M62 near Adwalton and Drighlington. I then embarked on an epic half-hour tour of three roundabouts and a McDonald's car park. I think I may well have discovered some loop in the space-time continuum that day because, no matter which way I turned, no matter which exit I took, I ended up back at McDonald's.

Pete was in his element. With every McDonald's stop and subsequent map-squint, he was bounding off for another double-cheeseburger. I was struggling to find anything resembling a battlefield on this huge intersection of roads. I'm still not sure how I found my way off that roundabout system but I think, at some point, I picked up enough speed to be hurled out of orbit. The extra weight of a thousand cheeseburger wrappers and Pete's bulging beef-belly may also have contributed to our reaching escape velocity. Whatever . . . one moment I was in the middle of a complicated road system, the next I was cruising at warp-8 into the small town of Drighlington.

I pulled up at a small library on the edge of some moorland, and began studying my OS map. After five minutes' careful calculations, I deduced we were in completely the wrong place. I needed to drive at least another couple of miles. Then I saw it.

Glancing out of my side window as I turned the

ignition key I spotted a large stone bearing a memorial plate.

'I wondered when you'd notice that,' said Pete. 'You're not much cop at spotting the old memorials, are you?'

'Why didn't you tell me? I was about to drive away.'

'I fancied another cheeseburger.'

Finding myself unable to speak without swearing, I hopped out of the car and made for the stone. It wasn't exactly a monument. It was a battlefield marker. Not only that, it claimed to be one of four battlefield markers. The information displayed was breathtaking . . . well, breathtaking for somebody like me. The stone described itself as Station One, and told me that I was standing on Adwalton Moor, which was a handy place to be standing but didn't say much for my map-reading skills. Up on a ridge to my left, it continued, had been the Royalist gun positions. I looked left. There was indeed a ridge, around 300 yards away and rising to meet the main road. Away to my right, just beyond a line of houses on the edge of the moor, lay the Parliamentarians. I looked at the row of houses. Then I looked back at the ridge, then at the houses, then at the ridge, then at the houses. Although giving passers-by the impression I was watching a game of long-distance-invisible-tennis, I was actually getting my bearings while recovering from a mild bout of shock. I'd expected Adwalton Moor to be unclear and confusing. Instead, I'd been at the battlefield two minutes and already knew exactly where the two armies were deployed.

The stone went on to suggest I check the library

information board before taking a walk around the other three markers. I did everything the stone told me to. I always do everything stones tell me to do.

I read the library board, which gave a full description of the day's hostilities. I'd read around ten Internet accounts and many textbook versions, but none described the battle as clearly as Drighlington Library's information board. My mind full of battle facts, I paced away across the moor and up the ridge to Station Two.

Station Two told me that I was standing among the Royalist guns, which I already knew because Station One had told me. I avoided being smug and telling Station Two, and read on.

Away to my left and right, it said, I'd have been able to see bodies of Royalist pikemen (I presumed this meant bodies as in groups rather than corpses – depends on the time of day I suppose).

It then informed me of the exact location of Parliament's lines from where I stood. I glanced at that row of houses again, shuffled my feet and suppressed a further smug grin. Then I looked at the houses again. Across the moorland and football pitches, behind that row of houses stood 4,000 Parliamentarians. Here, where I stood, spread out all around me, were 10,000 Royalists.

Battle was about to commence.

In all truth, by the time these positions were occupied, it had already started – when the two armies walked slap-bang into each other on the Howley Hall to Bradford road.

The advance guards had met and clashed, and the Royalists were driven back. Accounts of these early skirmishes bring to mind two cartoon armies on long lengths of elastic: the Royalists were driven all the way back to their own advancing lines then TWANG! the pursuing Parliamentarians took one look at the 10,000 men they'd run into and got chased by a number of Royalists all the way back to *their* advancing army and TWANG! the Royalists ran into 4,000 Parliamentarians and went hurtling back whence they came.

But that was it for light-hearted animations and playful bungee games. The Parliamentarians deployed on a hill (behind the present-day houses) and watched the numerically superior Royalists take up battle positions on the moor below them. It was time for some serious fighting. Of course, those that had been killed during the initial exchanges could argue that the fighting had already got a bit serious.

I was about to set off to Station Three, but noticed a large man frantically waving at me from the moorland beside Drighlington Library. It was indeed time for a pint.

A quick drive around the moor's perimeter showed us that the battlefield of Adwalton Moor is home to only one pub, named the Railway. Pete almost ran through its door; I followed backwards, staring across the landscape as I went.

The Railway is a big open-plan pub, nicely decorated in a trendy, modern fashion with red walls, light pine tables and chequered seats. Nicely decorated, if you like that sort of thing. It's not the sort of place you'd expect to be big on war memorabilia, but it did have a framed photograph of a battle re-enactment on the moor, along with a brief description of the original. I stood and read it as Pete got the drinks in. He chose two pints of Black Sheep, then remembered I'd want a drink too.

I've always liked the story behind the naming of Black Sheep Ale. It's brewed by Paul Theakston of the famous Theakston's brewing family. There had been differences of opinion in the family, and eventually Paul broke away from the business and brewed his own beers; the first (along with the brewery) being named Black Sheep, for he was now, after all, the black sheep of the family.

Having said this, I've also read that he called it Black Sheep because the area has lots of sheep. Another article said it was named Black Sheep because Robert Theakston took out a lease on the Black Bull Inn in 1827 (why not the Black Bull Brewery, then?). It depends which beer-festival pamphlet you read. I don't care which is true. I like the first one, so I'll believe that.

As I dragged myself from the Railway's one piece of Civil War memorabilia and walked to the bar, Pete plonked a half-pint of John Smith's in front of me. 'Special offer on the Smith's,' he explained, sipping his Black Sheep. I noted with alarm that he'd also ordered two packets of peanuts and so, not having packed my goggles, moved my bar stool back a foot or two.

The pub was empty but for a middle-aged couple at a nearby table. They didn't stand a chance. Pete was on them like a praying mantis – happily telling them all about our trip, our trip's purpose, and cheeseburgers. They seemed delighted, inviting us to join them and introducing themselves in that way people from the North of England seem to find so much easier than most of us in the South. Bar Pete. Barbara had been a history teacher before retirement and knew everything there was to know about the Civil War and, specifically, the Battle of Adwalton Moor. We chatted for half an hour, while Pete sat happily listening in silence and consuming as much beer and nuts as humanly possible.

The conversation was fascinating. They told me all about a book named *The Forgotten Battle*, which many people consider Adwalton Moor to be. There's truth in this. Considering the battle's size and relevance, Adwalton Moor doesn't seem to have the historical prominence it deserves.

The battle was the first large-scale confrontation of 1643 and the biggest since Edgehill, and yet when we recount Civil War battles it is so often brushed aside or – as the title of the book bemoans – forgotten. Barbara also gave me the phone number of the undisputed local expert on the subject. These were quite definitely the right people to bump into on the edge of a battlefield.

As the conversation progressed, and my reasons for visiting battlefields were revealed to be as much 'pub' as 'history', Pete finally offered a further contribution, and it was one for which I'd have probably hit him had he not been wearing glasses (one at his mouth and one clutched to his chest).

'He's the right sort of bloke to write an historical travelogue is our Chris [slipping effortlessly into northern phraseology]. His other books were about a cat falling over!'

The couple laughed, but Pete hadn't finished.

'How's that for a contrast, eh? One minute he's writing about a crazy cat riding car roofs and catching fire, the next he's doing blood and guts and war. Mental, absolutely mental!'

Barbara, at least, took an interest. 'What were your books called, Chris?'

'*A Cat Called Birmingham*,' boomed Pete, laughing aloud and throwing a handful of nuts into his merrily beaming mouth, 'that was the first!'

'Really? I've read that. So you're Chris . . . Pascoe? Is it Pascoe?'

Peanuts spilled abruptly from Pete's mouth. I too choked upon my beer. Somebody had heard of one of my books. Somebody had actually heard of *A Cat Called Birmingham*. For the first time, I'd met somebody outside of my acquaintances who'd actually read it. I was speechless; I felt like asking for Barbara's autograph.

'Wait till I tell my friend I met you!' she continued. 'She's got it too. And the sequel.'

Pete's shocked intake of breath broke the silence.

Whether because they now knew who I was and wanted to get away quickly or they genuinely had other things to do, Barbara and her husband soon said goodbye and wandered off down the road. Pete watched them go, shaking his head in wonder.

'Unbelievable. She's read your books. That's amazing, isn't it?'

I instantly became defensive. 'Look, sales were absolutely fine. Somebody had to have read them!'

'Yeah,' said Pete reflectively, 'I suppose somebody had to . . . '

I was by now onto Diet Cokes, and Pete was half-cut, so I decided it was time to get back into the field. Pete was in no mood to leave his bar stool. As I paced back to the battlefield alone, I resolved to make sure I tripped Pete over the moment he'd had enough drinks to assume he'd collapsed.

I went off in search of Station Three. I searched and I searched. Eventually I saw a promising-looking stone in the distance, across from the moorland on an adjacent rugby pitch. After plodding over the muddy pitch, I was baffled to find that it read only 'Battlefields 2004'. On its reverse were some initials that looked very much like the name of a rugby club. This was a marker of sorts (I think) but it wasn't Station Three. Station Three seemed to be missing.

I walked back across the moor to Drighlington Library from where, as fortune would have it, the couple from the pub were just emerging. They pointed to the side of the moor I'd just come from, and told me it was further out than where I'd been looking. I spent another hour walking, but never found the third marker. I asked various people along the way, but nobody else knew where it was.

Enough was enough. I'd have to find it another day. I could see Station Four in the distance and that's where I was heading – because Station Four stood in front of the row of houses, and something momentous happened at Station Four.

After the initial shenanigans of that summer day

in 1643, Fairfax split his Parliamentarian army into two groups of around 1,200 musketeers and five troops of cavalry (around 350 men), positioned on either flank, the right flank commanded by his son, Sir Thomas Fairfax. In reserve, under his own command, were between 500 and 600 musketeers and a large contingent of makeshift-weapon-wielding locals.

Newcastle's cannon faced them from the ridge opposite. In front of the cannon, on lower ground, were the musketeers. Left and right of the musketeers were the pikemen, and beyond them the 4,000 horse cavalry.

The battle opened with Royalist aggression. Cannon fire roared over the heads of the Royalist muskets and into the Parliamentarian lines, while troops of Royalist horse galloped forward to attack Thomas Fairfax's heavily outnumbered right wing. But the Parliamentarians held out, peppering the attacking Royalist cavalry with flanking fire and driving them back as soon as they reached Sir Thomas's troopers.

The Royalist cavalry charged again with the same result. Or at least, almost the same result. Things went from bad to worse for the attacking Royalists. Thomas Fairfax's cavalry met them with a ferocious counter-charge that not only repelled them but drove them all the way back to their own artillery lines.

And things were going no better for Newcastle's men elsewhere on the field, each advance being forced back by Parliamentarian musketeers. Despite their huge numerical advantage, the Royalists were losing the battle. With casualties mounting and no breakthrough in sight,

Newcastle had to admit defeat and issued orders to withdraw.

But there was one Royalist officer who didn't like that idea at all. Having spent the last several hours being repeatedly mauled by the enemy, he wanted more of the same. With an attitude like his, it's not surprising that his name was Posthumous. Sir Posthumous Kirton, to be precise. A name just made for someone determined to die in battle. On hearing Newcastle's plans to retreat, Sir Posthumous asked permission to lead a body of pikemen (all of whom no doubt expected to soon have 'posthumous' linked to their names in some way) in one final attack on Parliament's musketeers.

Not wishing to spoil Sir Posthumous Kirton's day, Newcastle gave his permission and settled back to watch his brave nutter of an officer march straight at the Parliamentarian lines, and presumably die. But Kirton had other ideas.

His furious headlong assault showed no signs of stopping as it ploughed straight into musket fire. Parliament's musketeers, who had held so solidly all day, were pushed further and further back until, finally, they broke. Newcastle, no doubt in mild disbelief, ordered his right wing of cavalry forward to capitalise on Kirton's success. The entire left wing of the Parliamentarian army collapsed.

I reached Station Four. It was right here, at Station Four, that Parliament's musketeers broke under Sir Posthumous Kirton's onslaught. With their lines in disarray and the Royalist cavalry bearing down on them, the Parliamentarians fled the field and, along with Lord

Fairfax's reserves, retreated to Bradford as fast as they could.

I looked over to my right, to the rugby pitch and bordering factory. Somewhere over there on Parliament's right wing, Sir Thomas was still holding out, but due to the lie of the land had no idea of the catastrophe that had befallen the army's left. He continued to fight on, unaware that he now had no protection on his flank and that his escape route to Bradford was under Royalist control. When news of his extremely precarious situation finally reached him, he ordered a full retreat in the only direction available to him; away from Bradford. The Parliamentarian army had been split in two.

From the Royalists' gun positions on the ridge ahead staggered a drunken fat man. Pete had left the Railway and was out on the moor. Not a promising sign. If he felt he'd had enough to drink then he'd *really* had enough.

He was waving at me frantically, pointing in the general direction of the pub. He appeared to be shouting at the top of his voice, but with the wind and traffic noise I could hear absolutely nothing. I began walking towards him. He stayed rooted to the spot, waving his arms, silently shouting and pointing towards the pub.

'What's the matter?' I called, when finally close enough to be heard.

'Phone,' he yelled back. 'Phone call for you.'

'What? In the pub?'

'Yeah, it's your missus.'

'On the pub phone? How did she know . . . ?'

'No, no, not the pub phone, you moron. On your mobile!'

My mobile? I tapped my pocket. Sure enough, no mobile.

I held out my hand as I reached him. He stared blankly at it.

'What?' he asked, genuinely bemused.

'My phone.'

'Your phone? It's in the pub.'

'Are you joking? Why didn't you bring it with you, you idiot?'

But Pete was already pacing back towards the pub. There comes a point, I think, at around five or six pints when that man's common sense drowns in a sea of best bitter.

I walked back into the warmth of the pub to see my mobile sitting alone on the bar. Lorraine had had the sense to hang up. I called her back.

'Hi, you wanted me?'

'No.'

'No? Pete told me you called.'

'No. Pete called me.'

'Pete called you?'

'Yes.'

'Why?'

'I have absolutely no idea.'

'Didn't he say?'

'Not really. He said a lot of things but it sounded like nonsense. There was something about a dog called Dave that he met in a pub and who's taking you to a nightclub, and something else about a lady who'd read your books.'

'Why is it nonsense that someone should have read my books?' I countered.

Lorraine ignored me. 'Then I asked to have a word with you and he said he'd go and get you. That was a quarter of an hour ago.'

After a quick chat I said goodbye and stared long and hard at Pete, who was back on his bar stool and chatting happily to the barman. Pillock.

I sat for a moment and contemplated my next move. Should I drive around the outskirts of Adwalton Moor in one last attempt to find Station Three, or call it a day? I was fairly sure that Station Three would simply mark Sir Thomas Fairfax's position, and so, with time getting on, the bright lights of Leeds beckoning, and the fact that Pete was still in the pub and not getting any soberer, I reluctantly decided to pour him into the car and head for Dave's. And Dave's.

I have rarely seen a barman look so relieved as the one who watched Pete stagger from the Railway that afternoon. Pete had talked him into the optics. The man looked utterly shattered. Pete did his regular post-pub trick of passing out upon hitting the passenger seat, and I was left to navigate my way back to Dave's house alone. He'd done his bit though. He'd introduced me to a couple I'd never have met without him. I decided to let him sleep peacefully, and not draw all over his face in marker pen.

Dave was pleased to see us, jumping up and licking our faces as we walked up the drive, while Dave the dog watched solemnly from the window. We were shown to our room, which had been kindly evacuated of young children, and as Pete snored on his single bed, I got ready for a big night out. I had to admit that after a long day driving, battlefield visiting and note-taking, I was really looking forward to hitting the bars of Leeds city centre.

Two hours later I sat staring at a bow-tied bingo caller named Dave in Dave's local working men's club. I consumed pint after pint of John Smith's while Pete, Dave, Dave's wife Jean, and their three daughters (none of them named Dave) sat listening to MC Dave and ticking off numbers on bingo cards. Dog Dave was back at the house. At around nine-thirty, the bingo was over, the multicoloured flashing disco lights came on and I found myself being dragged onto the dance floor by an eighty-year-old woman named Dave. Actually, I don't know for sure that her name was Dave, but I assume it was. Pete, who after his power naps seemed as right as rain, had wasted no time in getting into the party mood and was swinging a woman who looked like my dance-partner's grandmother in an extremely dangerous fashion.

With the 'bright lights of Leeds' just a few miles to the north, I ended up spending the entire night valiantly attempting to get off a working men's club's dance floor. Near the end of the evening, I remembered something that had bothered me earlier in the day.

I cornered our kind hostess Jean at the bar, and asked her about the dog. Dave seemed a well-behaved dog, so just why was it that Ben decided he could no longer cope with him and sent him north. Over thumping disco music and the whoops of happy revellers, I caught only half of Jean's reply.

'Eating . . . shoes . . . locked in shed . . . ate shed.'

Ate shed? This seemed to confirm Pete's sketchy memories on the subject.

'How do you eat a shed?' I yelled back.

'Keep chewing!' yelled Jean. 'He just sort of started with a hole in the wall and just kept on chewing. Ben loved that shed.'

More crazed OAP-forced dancing followed. By the time we staggered home clutching chips and kebabs, I was totally knackered. But happily so. It had been an interesting day. Adwalton Moor had been a surprise. A historical site that I'd assumed would be little more than a memory amongst housing estates had turned out, for me, to be the Disneyworld of battlefields. So thoughtfully had the markers been placed and worded, you couldn't help but picture the dramatic events of that bloody day in 1643. Unless, of course, you'd stayed in the pub all day.

The battle's result had been Royalist control of Yorkshire. Sir Thomas Fairfax, who fought so gallantly throughout the day, led his tired troops on a night march after the battle, eventually linking up with his father in Bradford and reuniting the army. But it was of little help to Bradford, which was taken after a brief morning bombardment. The Parliamentarian army fled first to Leeds, and then to the relative safety of Hull. In Yorkshire, as in the rest of the country, things were not going well for Parliament.

But at least the 'Forgotten Battle' did not take place on a forgotten battlefield. And Adwalton Moor, while not springing readily to most people's minds, is at least remembered in the histories of the war. Which is not the case with all battles.

I was soon to discover the surprising truth about a battle that truly had been forgotten.

Totally forgotten. Or . . . had there been a battle at all?

The War outside
My Window

In which the Author convinces a young couple that he's a very 'special' person indeed

'BLAHHH!' said the voice at the other end of my mobile.

'Pardon,' I replied, checking the phone screen to see who was shouting.

'BLAHHH, FALCON, BLAHHH, RYE, HEH-HEH!'

The line went dead. 'Pillock's mobile', read the display. The display was the only thing that made sense. I stared out of the call-centre window on a crisp and sunny winter afternoon. I spend a lot of time staring out of the call centre's windows. My actual job is to ring lots of people and ask them to complete seemingly pointless surveys, and this I do, but I would do it much better and irritate far more people if I didn't spend my time writing up book notes and staring out of windows.

The usual object of my faraway gaze was the Rye,

a small area of green fields just the other side of the road in my home town of High Wycombe, stretching away to the River Wye on its far side. Pete had definitely shouted 'Rye'. I squinted from my window but could see no large shape with a mobile phone waving at me from the field. He'd also said 'Falcon'. I checked the time. Three-thirty on a Thursday afternoon. The likelihood that Pete would have knocked off work early to walk across the Rye was fanciful at best. The chances of him being in the Falcon, a pub in the town centre, were high.

My phone rang again.

'BLAHHH, SIGNAL SHIT, BLAHHH, LISTEN FALCON BATTLE!'

The line fell silent again. Battle? Was he taking an interest in my Civil War research at last?

Or was he involved in a fight in the Falcon? Or had he arranged for someone in the Falcon to fight me in a bare-knuckle boxing match on the Rye?

The last scenario made use of every audible word and therefore the most sense. The general annoyance we were causing each other on our trips was probably still at a level where an organised beating might be arranged. I somehow resisted the urge to leave work early and leg it, regardless of how many bets Pete had taken on me going down in the first round. Instead, I rang the Falcon pub and asked if there was a noisy bloke at the bar drinking their strongest beer much too fast. After a series of raucous shouts, Pete came on the line.

'Yeah, you'll never believe it, battle right here, on the Rye. On the bloody Rye. Civil War battle. Prince Rupert, the works . . . '

'What?' I asked, gobsmacked. 'What battle on the Rye? There was no battle on the Rye.'

At this point my mind was racing. I knew all the Civil War battles, didn't I? Surely there was never a battle here, in my home town. As far as I knew, Wycombe's only Civil War involvement had been a very minor Royalist raid to the west of the town in 1643, notable only because it caused a bit of a panic at the time. The raiding party had managed to get between Essex's army and London, making everybody feel a little vulnerable. But this had been merely a looting exercise, a ransacking of known Parliamentarians' homes – not a battle.

Could there be any truth whatsoever in Pete's words? Had I been travelling the length and breadth of the country visiting battle sites when one had taken place right here, outside my window? Never. As much as I wanted to believe it, I was well aware that Pete's early inputs in the field had been less than encouraging. Not only had he insisted that the Battle of Stamford Bridge (1066, Yorkshire, Saxons vs Vikings) was a decisive English Civil War battle, he also insisted it had taken place on Chelsea FC's ground. Someone had told him so in the pub, so it had to be true. No argument would convince him otherwise.

The shouting continued a little while longer, Pete competing with background noise from the bar. I imagined him standing there, shouting his head off in the pub, raving on about Roundheads and Cavaliers on the Rye. Probably standing above some poor, shaken couple's table. Through the sudden urge to hear more of

Pete's surprising news, and for the general wellbeing of the imaginary couple, I told Pete I'd be in the pub in twenty minutes and hung up.

The beauty of my job in the call centre is that I'm so utterly expendable I can leave whenever I like. No one cares in the slightest whether I'm there or not. Twenty minutes later I walked into the Falcon and found Pete, unbelievably, leaning over a shaken couple's table. On the wall behind the couple was a framed drawing of Civil War pikemen containing a few lines of text.

'There, see!' boomed Pete, causing the pair at the table to jump out of their skins.

I smiled a slightly embarrassed hello to the couple, asked if it would be OK if I read the print behind them, and then joined Pete leaning across their table. I stared at the text and could barely take in what I was reading:

> In 1642, a battle took place on the open land known as the Rye. Four thousand pikemen commanded by Captain Hayes beat off an attack by Lord Wentworth's troops.

A bloody battle

> The fighting lasted several hours in which an estimated 900 of Wentworth's royalist troops were killed. Around 300 of Parliament's soldiers were killed defending the town, which was an important military base for Parliament during the Civil War.

This was incredible. Not only was this one of the opening skirmishes of the war, it was no small affair. With 4,000 Parliamentarian pikemen involved, this was one of the larger skirmishes. But how many Royalists had fought here? The print didn't say. If their numbers had equalled those of Parliament we were talking about a substantial battle. And the casualties! The losing Royalists had lost a catastrophic 900 men. At Edgehill, Parliament had suffered the battle's greater losses and lost around 10 per cent of their soldiers. If Royalist participants on the Rye had indeed equalled Parliament's, then they'd suffered more than 20 per cent.

And it seemed that they hadn't gone down without a determined fight, taking 300 Parliamentarians with them. This had been bloody in the extreme. A massacre. An English Civil War massacre had occurred on a stretch of grassland that I'd been idly staring at for most of the last few years. I'd frequently ambled across that grass during the summer months. I'd had absolutely no idea what had happened there.

It is moments like these that send you drifting into a world of your own. For maybe two or three minutes my mind drifted, imagining the yells of battle and the clash of steel against steel out there on the Rye.

The moment you arrive back from that world of your own can often be the most embarrassing. To snap back to full consciousness and find yourself leaning heavily across a table with your jaw hanging wide open and your eyes glazed is bad enough for the mind-drifter. But it was much worse for the couple at the table, whose previously pleasant view of one another had deteriorated into nothing more than a few stolen glimpses around my head. I stood bolt upright, alarming them further still. Mumbling a heartfelt apology, I backed away from their table, noting that Pete was now fifteen feet away and helpless with laughter. I walked over to him and stood in silence, waiting for him to calm down. An hour later, it was obvious he wasn't going to. One by one, various acquaintances arrived and, one by one, they were enter-tained by Pete's rendition of the 'loony upsetting the poor couple' story. By the fourth telling, I'd not only been leaning between the couple, but drooling and mumbling profanities to myself.

I was by now on a third pint of Old Speckled Hen, and so just didn't care. Neither did I care much for the name 'Old Speckled Hen', and haven't called it that in years. It sounds very much like a serious farmyard medical condition, and as such its local nickname is Fowlpest, and always will be for me. In actual fact, the correct name has nothing to do with chickens or diseases at all. It was brewed to commemorate the fiftieth anniversary of the MG factory in Abingdon and named after a paint-spattered MG car that used to drive around the factory, affectionately known by workers as the Owd Speckled 'Un. A very strange naming process, but who cares – it was going down extremely well, if possibly a little too quickly.

The couple had long since departed, smiling goodbye to me as they left, and although my instinct had been to follow them out and offer one more sincere apology for my behaviour, Pete had pulled me back and hastily reminded me of the Lisbon incident, insisting that I'd 'done enough damage already'. One other instinctive reaction of mine was also battered down by Pete, this time with a pre-emptive strike. I'd fully intended to walk back down to the Rye, but before I'd even aired my plans, the deriding 'Don't tell me you're going to go and stare at the *Rye* now! You've stared at that enough, haven't you?' put me right off.

So I decided to stay in the pub. Wycombe is a fairly decent town to go out drinking in, with lots of pubs in a small area. A decent town to go out drinking in, as long as you're not with Pete Ilic. Unfortunately I was and so, three hours later, having rolled from the Falcon to the cosy and dimly lit Hobgoblin, swiftly on to the Antelope (once the home of the Royal Military College) and then through two of the town's super pubs to the small and friendly Bell, I was lying flat on my face in my hallway, totally unable to field Lorraine's questions on how I'd got into this state on a day I was supposedly working.

When I awoke the next day and somehow lurched back to the call centre, the elation of a battle on my doorstep had somewhat evaporated, and not only because of my desperate head situation. The cold reality finally hit me that, if there had indeed been a battle of the magnitude described on the pub wall-print, then surely I would have heard about it. There would be a monument on the Rye, an information board, crossed swords and '1642' printed on every decent road map. At the very least, there would be a lengthy entry in the town's standard history, but I had never seen any mention at all.

It was truly the morning after the night before. I realised I'd somehow taken a pub print to be definite proof of something for which I had absolutely no supporting evidence whatsoever. I briefly wondered if Pete had planted the print as a wind-up. I considered this very unlikely, far too elaborate for Pete, but in the midst of dispelling the thought, something else struck me. Prince Rupert. Well . . . no . . . Prince Rupert didn't strike me, although I'm sure he would have done had he met me. The thought struck me that Pete had mentioned Prince Rupert. Where had he got that from? There'd been nothing on the print about Rupert. The text had clearly stated that the Royalists were led by Lord Wentworth (not to be confused with the luckless and already dead Earl of Strafford, but one of Charles's trusted cavalry commanders, the son of Thomas Wentworth, the Earl of Cleveland). The plot thickened. I checked my call-centre supervisor was out of earshot and made two quick phone calls.

The first was to Wycombe Reference Library, who very kindly agreed to search their records for 'The Battle of the Rye', and the second was to my beer-guzzling friend whom I now suspected of fraud.

It is a testament to my befuddled, hung-over brain that morning that I called the library and risked ridicule *before* checking that I hadn't been the victim of a Falcon/Pete prank. Especially as, in all truth, I was by now totally convinced I'd been conned. My first words to Pete bore this out.

'Yeah, yeah, very funny, Pillock. Wycombe Library never heard of any "Battle of the Rye".'

The annoyingly healthy, un-hung-over voice on the end of my phone feigned surprise at my words. I continued, more and more convinced that none of this rang true.

'So, if it's not all a con, why did you say Prince Rupert was involved, eh, eh, why did you say Prince Rupert was involved?'

'Because a bloke in the pub told me [that made sense]. He said he read about it at Aylesbury Museum.'

I stole another quick glance towards my supervisor and made two further calls, the first to directory enquiries, the second to Aylesbury Museum. I was put through to a very helpful lady named Melanie who, to my total surprise, confirmed they did indeed have a display poster that mentioned a battle on Wycombe Rye. As she put me on hold and went off to read it, I sat shaking my head, my previous day's happy disbelief returning. Melanie returned to the phone. The poster apparently mentioned that Lord Wentworth had been involved in a battle on the Rye, and also stated that he'd fought alongside Rupert in other battles, including Chalgrove. Nowhere did it say that Rupert had been on the Rye, but it was easy to understand why the confusion had arisen.

So there had been a battle after all. Aylesbury Museum had no further information, and could not confirm the troop numbers shown in the Falcon. I was now desperate to get home and scour the Internet for details. Two days of simply walking out of the call centre during a working day seemed a bit off, so I decided I'd give my supervisor the option. I handled it as tactfully as I could.

'Do you mind if I go home?'

'No. Not at all.'

'Goodbye then.'

'Goodbye.'

And so Maritz UK's number-one pointless employee raced off home without having made a single customer call, and spent seven virtually fruitless hours on the Internet. There was little more than nothing to see. A local garage's website contained the line, 'The Rye, scene of a bloody Civil War battle in 1642 . . . ' but offered no more. I emailed the Sealed Knot, those meticulous Civil War battle re-enactors who bring the war to life so vividly at many battlefields, pageants, castles and fetes. They advised me to hang around their next beer tent and ask a few people, which was a great idea and one that Pete would have admired them for. I also contacted the local council's historical department. The historical people had never heard of a battle on the Rye, offering details only of the aforementioned minor raid. They also stated that they were extremely sceptical that any battle involving 1,200 casualties could possibly have occurred without demanding a significant place in the town records. They then suggested I contact Wycombe Reference Library, so, by the end of the day, I was back to square one.

Over the next week it became clear that finding any further details was going to be extremely difficult. The few websites that mentioned the Rye did so as nothing more than a passing comment. None offered battle details, numbers or casualty figures. The staff at the Falcon pub were unable to tell me where they'd obtained the print, not because the information was classified but because they had no idea, although taking into account the tight-lipped 'There's a war on, you know' attitude of a certain pub in Kineton, maybe pubs were just unwilling to supply information to any possible enemy. There could be something in that. Maybe pubs, often having been coaching inns or the like way back in Civil War days, still held the unimaginable fear experienced by the average inhabitant of a war-torn and blood-soaked England within those old walls and foundations, passing that intense insecurity and suspicion of strangers to all those that now worked behind their bars. Or probably not. Probably the staff just didn't know.

I was at an impasse. My own Civil War battle, the battle outside my window, was going to have to remain shrouded in the mists of time. The Rye's two adjacent pubs would now never be able to join my battlefield list. Not when the fight on the Rye seemed to have been, judging by the sheer lack of local historical records, probably little more than a minor skirmish. Not that either pub would probably have cared much either way: 'Oh, sod it, you mean the battle we've never heard of didn't actually happen? That's a blow.' The Pheasant, at the east end of the Rye, is a pub Pete and I have had a pint in many times. It's a fairly standard affair: one large room, low-lit and carpeted at one end, brightly lit and centring around a pool table and large TV at the other. The Pride is a gay pub, which I'd never visited, but I was surprised to learn that Pete had.

'Why?' I enquired.

'Because it's a pub,' came the answer.

'But it's a gay pub. You're not gay.'

'Ah, but they don't ask you that when you walk in, do they?'

'But why would you want to go in a gay pub?'

'Well, the beer's not gay, is it?'

'Well, no . . .'

'And I don't think they limit themselves to serving gay food.'

Feeling suitably stupid and admonished, I dropped the subject. It mattered little anyway, as the Pride didn't occupy the edge of a known 'proper' battle site any more, and so couldn't feature in my book.

But then, suddenly, everything changed. I received a call from Wycombe Library. They had in their hands two envelopes full of papers that seemed to confirm everything I'd told them. These papers were known by the *X Files*-style name of 'the green papers', and I couldn't wait to read them.

I raced down to the library, found a seat and launched into stacks of photocopied, very un-green papers. It was all true. Everything the Falcon print had claimed was true, except for one thing. The battle was even bigger than claimed.

In 1642, Wycombe had occupied a key strategic position. The surrounding Chiltern Hills, on London's doorstep, meant a lot to both sides and Parliament was determined to hold the area in defence of the capital. Wycombe became a major storage centre and a training ground for Parliamentarian recruits. Defensive garrisons were set up in the surrounding towns of Wendover, Amersham, Chesham and Aylesbury. To the south

Wycombe was defended by a Parliamentarian force at Windsor Castle.

Wycombe's first alarm came shortly after Edgehill, amid rumours that the Royalists were marching on London and Wycombe was in the way. That attack never materialised, but one came less than two months later. And it was quite an attack.

Only days before the Battle of the Rye, the Earl of Essex had been in Wycombe ensuring that its defences were sufficient – which was probably a contributory factor in 5,000 Royalist troops managing to waltz in unhindered. Five thousand! I couldn't believe the numbers I was reading. Only 2,000 Royalists had been involved in the far better known battle of Chalgrove Field, yet 5,000 Royalist horse under Lord Wentworth departed Oxford on 6 December 1642, with the intent of launching a surprise attack on Wycombe.

But Wentworth's idea of a surprise attack was straight from the Prince Rupert school of deft manoeuvres. Through the local village of Penn they came, thousands of cheering horsemen, towing clattering artillery pieces, blasting their trumpets and generally drawing attention to themselves. Word reached Wycombe before they did, and while they entered the town unopposed, opposition within the town had positioned itself well.

Four thousand Parliamentarian pikemen under Captain Hayes spread out across the Rye on the very stretch visible from my window. In fact, I'd assume their lines would have extended through the building I work in, the future Maritz UK call centre, and well beyond.

On their flanks were a large contingent of untrained locals and a small number of dragoons.

From the east side of the Rye, advancing through the current car park and outdoor swimming pool, came Wentworth's cavalry. The two sides faced one another across the Rye. Around 10,000 men on Wycombe Rye, ready to do battle. Wentworth had more in common with Rupert than just a scant regard for surprise tactics. He decided to ignore the artillery he'd just towed thirty miles across country and, in a move Rupert would have been proud of, ordered a trumpet fanfare and charged straight at the Parliamentarian lines.

The papers in my hand recorded little of the ensuing bloodbath. Written accounts state only that the Royalists hurled themselves against their foes, were repelled, and then, as they attempted to recoil, were set about with fury by the ill-trained rustics at their flanks. The Royalists sustained 900 casualties and Lord Wentworth was wounded. Many more Royalists were taken prisoner. The Parliamentarians later reported that 300 of their own men had been killed.

The shattered Royalist cavalry left the scene in any direction they could, some towards Henley, while others made for Aylesbury. Cannonballs found in neighbouring villages suggest they had to endure further fights along the way.

From Wycombe Library I took the short walk to the Rye as if in a dream. I was going to stand on the Rye and stare after all.

A few days later, it dawned on me that I would have to visit the Pride public house.

It was now officially a pub on, yes, actually *on*, a major battlefield and so well deserving of a visit from myself and Pete. Well . . . few pubs have actually done anything bad enough to 'deserve' a visit from Peter Ilic, but they were getting one anyway.

Or were they? Fourteen days later, the visit still hadn't been made.

'I don't know what you're so worried about. It's not as if you're homophobic or anything. It's just a ruddy pub!'

Those uncharacteristically wise words from Pete were totally true, but three times over the past fortnight, I'd bottled out of visiting the Pride. I have no idea why I was nervous. I'm certainly *not* homophobic. I've worked with lots of gay people at the call centre, one of whom is a good friend of mine and someone I find easier to beat at pool than any person I know, which makes her all the more dear to me. I have no crappy, prejudiced views on any section of society, so I had no real reason to worry about going into a gay pub at all.

I think I may possibly have been so nervous because I'd only ever been in one gay bar before, on holiday, and the memory still haunts me. A friend of mine and I had walked around a cove from a Greek island beach to an adjoining beach named 'Super Paradise'. We went into the first bar we saw, which was much more Caribbean-style than Aegean – everybody sitting beneath palm fronds and drinking cocktails from coconut shells. I remember being quite surprised that every person in the place was male, and that each and every one of them was toned, tanned and faultlessly groomed. Even these heavy hints didn't break through my thick skull. Neither of us cottoned on to the fact we were in a gay bar until we stepped out on to the beach and found it to be under a thick carpet of completely naked, sunbathing men. It was then and only then that we realised we'd reached an area of Mykonos that was not really our cup of tea.

The sight was truly horrific to me. I've never seen so many penises in one place. It reminded me of the bucket of worms my dad used to take fishing. My friend and I glanced gravely at one another, and then silently marched on, avoiding the swathe of terror beneath our feet as we resolutely made our way to a waiting taxi-boat, which whisked us back to our girlfriends on the unisex beach we'd left behind.

So, based on that memory I would have to admit that the words 'gay bar' conjure up the image of 2,000 penises. Thankfully I've resisted the urge to mention this to Pete. He'd have probably decided that my marriage was a sham.

On my fifteenth day of Pride abstention, it suddenly occurred to me that I'd be better off visiting a gay pub with the aforementioned gay friend – a person naturally at ease in the place, and much less likely to cause any kind of embarrassing rumpus. Well . . . unless she mentioned her full name – Britney-May Tinkerton (hee-hee!!!). My new plan in mind, I called her on the phone:

'Hi, Britney-May. Do you fancy going for a drink later?'

'Hey, Chris, sure. [Britney-May speaks in strange American tongues.] You wanna go to Mr Q's?'

'No. How about the Pride?'

'The Pride? Why?'

'I need to go there.'

'You *need* to go to the Pride? Is there something you ain't been telling me?'

'What? No, no, nothing like that.'

'They ain't even got a pool table, Chris. Let's go to Mr Q's, OK?'

'I really want to go to the Pride. It's some research I'm doing.'

'Research? Yeah, well, if that's the sort of thing you're researching, just ask, OK? While we're playing pool in Mr Q's. See you there at six . . . ' Click.

I replaced my handset. That went well.

I decided to go along anyway. Maybe I could convince her to come with me to the Pride once I'd beaten her at pool. Both plans failed. I lost at pool, and she went home. It was eight o'clock, I'd drunk three pints of bitter and I still hadn't visited the Pride. It was time to call in the cavalry. I made a bar-to-bar phone call.

'Pete? Are you in the pub?'

'Of course I am.'

'Do you fancy going for a pint or two down the Pride?'

'The office.'

'Pardon?'

'The office.'

'No, the Pride, What's the office?'

'The Pride.'

'Yes . . . the Pride. Do – you – fancy – going – to – the – Pride?'

'The office.'

I shook my head in mild despair. What was the matter with this bloke? Why was it virtually impossible to have a normal conversation with him? Fortunately, Pete's next words prevented me disconnecting and heading home:

'The Pride's gone. Name's been changed. Two weeks ago. It's called the Office now.'

'Really?' I said, slightly surprised. Despite working a few doors down, I hadn't noticed. 'Is it still a gay pub?'

'I don't know, mate. We can find you a gay pub if you want one. Feeling a bit frisky, are you?'

I declined to dignify the remark with an answer and, fifteen minutes later, I met Pete beside the grand old battlefield of Wycombe Rye and, hand in hand, we climbed the stone steps to the Office's doors. Well . . . we climbed the steps, anyway. There was none of that 'hand in hand' business, thank you very much.

The pub turned out to be pretty cool. The bar is shaped like an American football and so close to the door you almost walk straight into it. In my case . . . you walk straight into it. The decor was bright and modern, with a long wall-table and stools down one side of the room.

Tables dotted the floor, and a DJ stage occupied one corner. Tall pot plants completed a picture of easy sophistication. Needless to say, there was nothing Civil War around but then, as our Wycombe battle is so badly documented, I didn't think there would be.

I knew Pete would embarrass me in a gay pub. There was no way he wouldn't. I nipped into the toilets while he ordered the drinks. When I came back, Pete was supping a bottled lager, but as I stepped to the bar I noticed a distinct lack of beer for me.

'Yours is just coming,' said Pete, smirking from ear to ear.

I'd just perched on a bar stool, when the barman unexpectedly shoved a huge piña colada into my hand, complete with multicoloured umbrellas, cocktail mixer sticks and a glacé cherry on top.

I stared at this stereotypical drink and felt my cheeks burning red. I couldn't even find my voice to swear. I then looked around at the rest of the bar's clientele. The place was buzzing with people, music and noise. There was a real energy in the atmosphere. But I, alone in the whole pub, was the only person so apparently gay as to be drinking a fluffy piña colada through a bendy straw.

A clearly inebriated chap leaned on the bar beside us.

'Are you a couple?' he asked.

I smiled and shook my head.

'Yes, we are,' said Pete, and put his hand on my shoulder.

'Oh,' said the chap, who then bought some crisps and rejoined his girlfriend at a nearby table.

It turned out there was a pool table in a back room. I could have come here with Britney-May after all. I'm sure there must be a Wycombe-wide conspiracy to ensure I go everywhere with Pete, and thus guarantee humiliation at every turn. Straight and gay, Cavalier and Roundhead, the world is against me.

We played a few games of pool, supped a few beers (and one cocktail), had a good time in what is probably the liveliest pub in Buckinghamshire, and left around 9.30 p.m.

I reached the door and realised Pete had been distracted en route, and was now happily watching two girls smooching beside a cigarette machine. I stepped outside to wait, looking across at the Rye, trying to drum up a little bit of Civil War atmosphere for myself as this was, after all, supposed to be a battlefield-pub experience.

After a few seconds I became aware that somebody was watching me. Looking down the steps, I saw my supervisor, who had evidently just left our call centre.

'Evening, Chris,' she called. 'I didn't know you drank in the Pride.'

'Oh, eh, no, not normally, I . . . '

At that moment a big gruff fat man named Pete burst through the doors behind me, grabbed my arm and, at the top of his voice, bellowed, 'C'mon then, lover, wait till I get you home.'

As I say, the world is against me.

Essex in Shirtsleeves – The First Battle of Newbury

In which the Author finds a little piece of Trafalgar in the wrong place, and is terrorised by geriatrics

Location! Location! Location! The battle of Newbury was all about that overused estate agent buzz-phrase.

After the now-familiar Civil War habit of toing and froing , the 15,000-strong Royalist army under King Charles found themselves near Newbury. Although they could easily be forgiven for having no idea how they'd got there, they were in fact there for a very good reason: namely that Essex's equally large Parliamentarian army were making their way back to London after nipping out to Gloucester. And Newbury seemed a nice spot to kill them.

Being first on the scene, the Royalists got to choose those aforementioned prized locations – where to deploy troops, how best to take advantage of their superior cavalry numbers, how to cover for their outnumbered infantry.

Having thought things through carefully, Charles, Rupert and co. chose to bugger up any chance of a crushing victory before the Roundheads even arrived. Gentlemanly lot, the Royalists. They chose an enclosed area awash with hedges and obstacles . . . an area ideal for infantry combat and a death-trap for cavalry. The complete opposite of their own requirements. Should have spoken to Kirstie and Phil.*

And, not only did they choose precisely the wrong battlefield, they chose to ignore said battlefield's only strategically important high ground – an elevated area known as Round Hill. What they did achieve, however, was to completely block Essex's route to London.

When the Parliamentarians arrived two hours later, at dusk, Essex saw the Royalist army splayed out before his tired and hungry men and no doubt muttered a few heartfelt expletives. There was no way through. The Royalists had blocked his path completely. Essex couldn't skirt north because he was blocked by the river Kennet, and he couldn't skirt south because the ground was too marshy.

The Parliamentarians bedded down for the night, knowing they were in for a big and inevitable fight in the morning. While his troops rested, Essex and his officers surveyed the landscape and, surprisingly, came up with a

---

* The famous TV property *Location Location Location* experts whom my wife insists we never, never miss. No disrespect intended, Kirstie and Phil, but I hate you.

plan. Imagine their shock and horror though, when from nowhere rattled a mud-covered Citreon C2 containing a pork-pie-munching fat man and a stressed-out author.

Well . . . they would have been shocked and horrified, had we not arrived three and a half centuries later.

'Which side do you think you'd have fought on in the Civil War?'

I glanced at my crumb-covered passenger in surprise. This was a rarity indeed – Pete starting a Civil War-related conversation. He was usually desperately trying to finish them.

'The Royalists!' I stated, without hesitation.

'NO WAY!' came the even less hesitant response.

'What? Why not?'

'The Cavaliers were dashing, brave, romantic . . . '

'All right, skip it, Pete.'

'You're a Roundhead, mate. Through and through.'

'Leave it.'

'A systemised, capricious little Roundhead.'

'Capricious?'

'Yeah, I'd say you were pretty capricious, yeah.'

'You don't know what capricious means, do you?'

'Of course I do.'

'What does it mean, then?'

'. . . I don't know . . . anyway, you just seem more Roundhead than Royalist to me.'

'Well, you're certainly more Cavalier.'

'Thank you.'

'It wasn't a compliment.'

'It was to me. I'm very much your dashing Cavalier type I reckon.'

'Well, they were a bunch of losers at the end of the day, weren't they, so I agree.'

Our drive around Newbury continued in silence.

More Roundhead than Royalist, eh? Cheeky git. But he had a point. I'd always sort of imagined myself fighting on the Royalist side, but then wouldn't most people? All that chivalry, colour and selfless gallantry? The courageous Cavaliers fighting bravely on as their comrades and their cause died around them. The Roundheads seemed so . . . grey, in comparison. And yet Pete was right. I suppose that despite my romantic notions, had I been around in the 1640s, I'd probably have been fighting for Parliament.

And, given my deftness of sword-hand and overall combat skills, dying quite quickly. But Pete – would he really have been fighting for Charles? Capricious, he'd called me. That's him, not me. Impulsive, prone to sudden changes of heart and attitude. He'd have fought for the Royalists certainly. Then the following week he'd have been fighting for Parliament. In fact he'd have fought for whichever side had the largest beer supply. And in war, beer stocks favour the victor, so Pete would undoubtedly have tailed off behind the beer wagon at the end of any battle – regardless who'd won.

As the sun rose on the morning of 20 September 1643, Essex set his plan into action. The Parliamentarian left wing unexpectedly attacked. The Royalists were so surprised to see somebody other than their own Rupert start a full-scale fight, they failed to notice Essex leading a large number of troops onto Round Hill. As the dust settled and the first action of the day abruptly ceased, the Royalists realised that Parliament were on the high ground, and that they'd somehow forgotten to occupy it themselves. Belatedly realising its artillery importance, the Royalists decided they'd have to shift their opponents immediately.

Thus started the real fighting.

The Royalists rushed forward several infantry regiments to take the hill. Essex, giddy with the excitement of having done something very clever indeed, cast off his uniform and stood ready to fight in his white shirtsleeves. This show of bold gallantry was surely enough to repel the hundreds of heavily armed Royalists charging towards him. The Royalist infantry charged through the Parliamentarian lines like a freight train. Essex's men were driven from the hill, and their pursuing enemy engaged them in confused and bitter fighting in the surrounding lanes.

But the Parliamentarians weren't finished yet. They regrouped, counter-charged and retook the hill. And this time they held it. Not only held it, in fact, but began advancing steadily forward from it. As Parliamentarian infantrymen pushed the Royalists back from Round Hill and down to the field below, known as Wash Common, they were joined by further infantry and cavalry. Suddenly they had a firm foothold on the field and pressed forward, threatening to forge a huge gap in the Royalist lines.

But Charles was quick enough to plug it, pouring forward infantry and cavalry. The Parliamentarians settled back to defend the ground they'd claimed. The battlefield of Newbury was set. Somehow, as full-scale hostilities broke out all around, Essex's Parliamentarian army had been allowed to seize all the advantages. Charles had made grave errors. But could his massed 6,000-strong cavalry, under Prince Rupert, overcome the perilous terrain and save the day for the King? Prince Rupert was always going to give it a go.

Like other battlefields before it, this one was proving rather difficult to locate. As Pete and I drove around, it became patently clear that there was something wrong with it.

Some idiot had placed the A34 Newbury Bypass and around a thousand houses on top of it. Finding even fragments of the battlefield was proving extremely problematic indeed.

The names of the streets on areas of the supposed field were encouraging enough, Battle Road, Charles Street, Essex Road to name but a few. But I couldn't even find any area of significant grass, let alone a field.

Finally we pulled up at a refreshingly huge monument. For once I was the one who spotted it. I think this was mainly due to the fact that it lay directly opposite two pubs. Pete's eyes didn't quite make it to the monument, even after I pointed it out. I knew exactly what Pete was about to say, so I threw the car into a parking space and jumped out the door before he could even breathe. Slamming the door in Pete's face, I turned quickly on my heels, narrowly avoided tripping over an elderly man in a wheelchair, and walked straight into oncoming traffic.

The car that hit me didn't really stand a chance. One moment I was nowhere to be seen, the next I was. Fortunately for me, the car was being driven by a lady of such advancing years that she made my Adwalton dance partner look like a mere child. The geriatric speed-king behind the wheel steamed into me at something approaching three miles per hour, slightly tapping my thigh. I glanced into her window, my eyes wide with surprise, and waved an apology, and also a heartfelt thank-you for having the foresight to drive so ridiculously slowly. By the chorus of beeps emanating from the mile-long queue of traffic on her rear bumper, I guessed that this appreciation was shared by many.

As I carried on across the road to the monument, I became acutely aware that the beeps were getting louder. I stopped beside the monument and looked over my shoulder. The elderly lady had abandoned her vehicle in the centre of the road and was shuffling towards me at an alarmingly slow pace.

I walked to the kerb to greet her. I must have waited near-on five minutes.

'I'm OK!' I called as she made her way towards me through a cacophony of car horns and angry shouts. 'No damage done, really, don't worry.'

She kept on coming.

'Shouldn't you go back to your car?'

She kept coming.

'You're blocking the road, you know.'

Still she came.

Finally, she made it. She looked me square in the eye.

'Oooo, sorry, love, I thought you were Jean's boy.'

'Eh, no,' I muttered.

'You're not a muck ridge are you?'

'A muck ridge?' Was that some kind of local insult? Or did she believe she'd ploughed off the road into some kind of talking mudbank?

'A Muckridge? You look soooo much like Jean Muckridge's boy. I thought, "That's Jean's boy waving at me over there, oooo, I'd better just stop and ask him how she's getting on." She had a hip replacement, you know. She wasn't right for a long while. Very nasty business.'

'Oh, right, I see. No, my name's Pascoe.'

Were those honks getting louder or was it my imagination? I could feel my stress levels rising. Dozens of angry faces shouted from open car windows. I began to sweat.

'Pascoe, is it? I'm Glenys. Pascoe . . . Pascoe. Hmm, I think I used to know a Pascoe. Fine old Cornish name, that is. Did you know that?'

'Er, I did, I think. Don't you think you should go back to your car? You're causing a bit of a jam. Sorry I stepped out in front of you like that. But you hardly hit me at all, I'm absolutely fine.'

Without really thinking, I began pushing gently on her shoulder, trying to turn her round. Two people were now out of their cars and waiting for a break in traffic to cross the road. She looked at my hand with interest, but didn't budge an inch.

'I hit you?' she asked, 'In my car? Did I? Oooo, I *am* sorry. I shouldn't be on the road, I really shouldn't.'

Two angry-looking men arrived at precisely that moment. They seemed to agree with her. I tried to explain that the whole thing was my fault, but my elderly friend was having none of it. She was a menace, she told us. Finally, with the help of the two aggressors, I shuffled Glenys the Menace back across the road and helped her into her car. The line of traffic sped off at two miles per hour.

I couldn't help but notice that my own car was now empty, and that a familiar bulky figure was disappearing through the door of the Old Bell public house. Typical. There were two pubs here, one of which boasted a hugely promising sign featuring Civil War soldiers firing a cannon, and . . . the Old Bell, which was so heavily draped in England flags that you could hardly see it.

I watched Pete pace urgently through the door, and turned my attentions to the monument. It was an odd one.

A Civil War monument should surely commemorate the dead of both sides. But this seemed a tad biased. In fact, totally biased. It was entirely pro-Royalist, talking of the heroics of the Royalist army, and the bravery of its commanders. It was as if the people who'd erected this monument had completely forgotten that the Parliamentarians fought here too. There was absolutely no mention of them. One part of the monument was devoted to the Royalists, the other to Lord Falkland of . . . the Royalists. Bizarre.

My mind far away, I stepped backwards into the road. The fact that I finished writing this book points strongly to the fact that I made it to the other side, but never in my life have I been so careless on one particular stretch of road. It was as if, due to my severe objections to it having been built on a battlefield, I refused to recognise its existence. Which, of course, is my right, but not one that should be exercised while crossing the said road, especially as most car drivers seem to have decided to let the matter go.

Turning, completing my crossing at a sprint and reaching the pavement to a further horn fanfare, I walked the hundred or so yards to join my single-minded friend in his pub-quest. I walked through the door and, to my sheer shock and bewilderment, was hit by a pensioner for the second time in a matter of minutes. What on earth was the matter with me today? I seemed to be charging around like a blind rhino in a minefield. And the owner of the Zimmer that smacked into my ankles was no better – he wasn't about to stop for anybody. He was leaving that pub through the door I was blocking, and that was that. Moving at a speed far greater than Glenys's, he shuffled forward and forward, driving me back through the door and out into the street. I stepped to move out of his way, but he turned with me. I found myself jammed against a railing, trying desperately to squeeze between metal on both sides as Zimmer-man pushed on through. And then he was gone, sauntering off down the road without so much as a backward glance. An extremely amused Pete stood in the pub doorway, pint in one hand, peanuts in the other. He shook his head, raised his eyebrows and held the door open for me.

'ALL CLEAR NOW!' he bellowed. 'In you come . . . be careful though.'

To say the Old Bell was not to my taste would be understating the case somewhat. A big bright room featuring televisions, more flags, a couple of glaring locals in chav caps, a pool table and Pete. The one small mercy was that the overpowering stench emanating from its open toilet door managed to take your mind off the rest of the place. Needless to say, Pete was in his element.

'What do you think?' asked my beaming friend, 'No Civil War crap at all, but nice little pub, isn't it?'

After a few moments' silence, I told Pete I'd wait outside, stepped back into the comparative relief of exhaust fumes and returned to the prejudiced monument. Studying it once more, I wondered again at the strangeness of a memorial in England honouring only one side of an all-English struggle. Had the Royalists done anything here to deserve such local support?

After the fight for Round Hill, the battle had settled into a familiar pattern. Parliament's pikemen formed defensive positions at the centre of the field, backed up by musketeers. The Royalists, once again, chose a cavalry offensive as a means to break them.

As so often before, Rupert's marvellously skilled cavalry troopers met their Roundhead counterparts on the field of battle and routed them totally, driving them into disorganised retreat. If the Civil War had been a cavalry-only war, by late 1643 Rupert would have won it for Charles and a lot of revolutionaries would have been swinging on ropes. But pikemen were becoming more and more organised. The breaking and running of Edgehill was a rarity, not least because running from a charging cavalryman proved to be a great way to die.

Infantrymen learned that their chances of survival lay in a solid formation, with pikes forward and a determination to hold. To break meant death. It was quite literally a case of united we stand, divided we fall.

With those terms of engagement, infantry were always going to be tough to break down. At Newbury this was especially the case, and not least because this really, really was NOT cavalry terrain. Behind every hedge and fence a Parliamentarian musketeer waited for the Royalist cavalry to charge.

When they did, it was a bloodbath.

Wave after wave of Royalist cavalry attack ended on the pikes of the iron pack. Cavalryman after cavalryman went down in hails of musket fire from all around. If the Royalists had any right to that singular monument here, it was for their sheer selfless bravery. Their task was hopeless. They charged over and over into the massed pikes, discharging their pistols at close range, swinging their swords at pikes but never reaching their holders, before finally being unsaddled by a well-timed jab or a carefully aimed musket ball.

Charles looked on as, one by one, his troopers died. All day they fought, never once coming close to breaking the enemy lines.

As darkness fell and the field fell silent, Charles faced some tough choices. Did he continue to stand in Essex's way in the morning? The advantages of stopping Essex reaching London were huge. This was Parliament's main field army. If it could be destroyed, the war was as good as won. But how to destroy it? How could he break it? His casualties were already high. How many more valuable troops would he lose attempting to break their seemingly impregnable defences for a second day running?

Charles made his decision. Under the cover of darkness, his army retreated. At Edgehill, a year before, Essex had moved aside and left Charles's road to the capital clear. Now Charles had returned the compliment. While there were no clear winners at Newbury – neither side had broken, neither side had progressed against the other – the day was seen as a symbolic victory for Essex, his first and only military success of the war. Newbury is often remembered as a turning point. For the first time, the King's men had totally failed in their objectives and been forced to leave the field with nothing whatsoever to show for their efforts. Things would get tougher still from now on, but Parliament had at last learned to match their opponents in battle.

Pete emerged from the green cloud behind me, a few pints better off and brandishing some good news. A chav had informed him of the whereabouts of the battlefield, and we were only a few minutes' walk from it.

Just around the corner from Wash Common's two pubs, we found it. Nestled between two main roads and the housing estate, on a small area of recreation ground with a playground, lay a section of the battlefield.

What set it apart from every battlefield I'd seen thus far was that it had two huge burial mounds slap-bang in the middle of it. Pete eyed them suspiciously.

'Are they burial mounds?'

'Yep.'

'They buried Civil War dead in burial mounds?'

'No. These must be from way before the Civil War.'

Pete strolled merrily onto one of the mounds, something I'm always reluctant to do. I don't like walking on anyone's grave, never mind graves in which any number of people may be buried. Pete didn't seem to be bothered at all. At the top of the mound he suddenly dropped to his knees. My automatic reaction was to assume he'd collapsed, but as he'd only had three pints so far, this seemed unlikely.

'Hey, Einstein!' he bellowed, studying something on the ground quite closely, 'you really know your stuff, don't you? There's a stone plaque up here, and listen to what it says: "Civil War. Sacred. To those who fell in the Battle of Newbury. September 20th, 1643."'

'Really!' I yelled, trampling over the dead as I climbed the mound at breakneck speed.

Stunning. Civil War dead buried here? In the middle of a recreation ground? I hurried to the second mound. Another stone plaque awaited me:

PEACE.
THIS STONE WAS PLACED ON THIS
SACRED SPOT
ON DIAMOND JUBILEE DAY 1897

I was quite honestly bemused. The Civil War habit had been to bury the dead where they fell or, if possible, get them to churchyards and bury them properly. Even in mass graves, they didn't build burial mounds. That tradition ended well before the Civil War, and went back to the days of Stonehenge and beyond. As much as I wanted to believe that these mounds contained Civil War dead (not because I've got anything against Civil War soldiers, you understand), it just didn't ring true at all.

I stood atop a great many dead people and thought long and hard. Not only did these mounds seem out of place, they were equally unexpected because in all my years of Civil War reading, I'd never seen anything about burial mounds at Newbury. A grotesque purple-hued bloated face suddenly appeared at my shoulder. For a moment I thought someone had escaped from the grave beneath my feet, but Pete generally looks this way after a short walk uphill. The face was gloating.

'Didn't have a clue about these mounds, did you. What was it . . . [insultingly dense voice] "These must be from way before the Civil War", ha ha.'

'Tosser.'

'Idiot.'

'Drunken fat git.'

'Not yet. When are we going to the Gun?'

'In a minute, I want to look round this battlefield first.'

'Battlefield? It's a bloody playground! A playground with *Civil War* mounds, that apparently don't exist.'

I ignored Pete's taunts and strode off across the field. It really didn't look up to much. The mounds aside, there was nothing to suggest anything of any note had ever happened in this place. So how did Newbury's planners remember such a hugely important event in

England's history? How did they commemorate the soldiers who lost their lives in this field? They dug most of it up, surrounded it with busy roads, built extensive housing all over it and left one tiny patch in the middle. Brilliant.

I then noticed an information board on the far side of the rec. At least they'd bothered to do *something*. It stood beside a public toilet and in front of a small copse of trees. Through the trees I could see an adjoining field. A little more battlefield than I'd initially thought.

But no more information than I'd thought. The board had absolutely nothing to do with a battle. Instead it related to the two burial mounds. Totally contradicting the stone plaques only two hundred yards away, it stated that the burial mounds were strongly suspected to have been built by Bronze Age people living in the area . . . quite a long time before the English Civil War.

I can only hope the plaques weren't offended, and only assume they were placed there due to a misplaced 1897 notion that the mounds possibly contained soldiers who died on this battlefield.

Then again, neither of the stones claimed their mounds actually *contained* Civil War casualties, did they? No, they merely commemorated them. I think the stone-layers may have been every bit as confused as Pete and I. They'd found huge mounds on a 1643 battlefield, thought them to be out of place, but bunged a couple of plaques on them anyway.

'PUB! PUB! PUB! PUB!' boomed a voice in my ear.

'In a minute, Pete, I'm just . . . '

'PUB! PUB! PUB! PUB!'

'Look, wait a sec, can't you . . .'

'PUB! PUB! PUB! PUB!'

The Gun, at least, was going to be a good one. With the best Civil War pub sign I'd ever seen, it was bound to be filled with battle memorabilia.

It certainly was. The Battle of Trafalgar.

The place was a shrine to Horatio Nelson and HMS *Victory*. I looked around the room absolutely aghast. Every wall boasted portraits of the Admiral and his famous ship. Every shelf contained a little memory of Trafalgar. Did the landlord not realise that the gunners on his sign were English Civil War gunners? Did he think they were in some way connected to an 1805 sea battle fought a thousand miles from our shores?

It's not that I'm not interested in Trafalgar. I've studied it extensively. Not least because my great-great-great-grandfather was Nelson's signals lieutenant on that fateful day. John Pascoe, in fact, was the very man responsible for the massively famous phrase, 'England expects every man will do his duty'. He was! Honestly.

Nelson has been accredited with it ever since, but what Nelson actually said was, 'Nelson confides* that every man will do his duty'. The battle was just starting when Nelson insisted this rallying call be broadcast to the fleet, so time was of the essence. Pascoe, therefore, suggested that the word 'England' replace 'Nelson', and

---

* The meaning of 'confide' in those days was slightly different. Nelson meant 'has confidence'.

'expects' replace 'confides', for these could be represented by just one flag, whereas the originals would have had to be spelled out with numerous flags.

So . . . it was *my* ancestor who coined that proud and patriotic battle cry, 'ENGLAND EXPECTS!'

How proud would he be to know that his great-great-great-grandson does virtually nothing in a call centre all day long, where his supervisor is a French girl who treats him with contempt? Not Very, I should think. But I was working on that. I was on a Mission.

So, I have a lot of time for Trafalgar, but . . . why here? Why remember Trafalgar here, in an area famous for a different war in a different century? I asked the barman this exact question, but his answering shrug revealed surprisingly little.

I also asked him why the pub had a Civil War sign but then ignored it. His shake of head and a second shrug cleared it all up for me. While the barman was of little help, and the pub clearly belonged in a dockyard somewhere, the overall experience was still a massive improvement on its nearby rival, being cosily and tastefully decorated and offering Adnams Broadside (brewed in honour of yet another sea battle – this one against the Dutch in 1672, only 29 years after the First Battle of Newbury, but a sea battle nonetheless . . . sigh) and good old land-based Fowlpest on tap.

Pete fared better with his own line of questioning, guzzling Fowlpest and striking up a conversation with four locals. The locals knew everything there was to know about the battlefield – virtually nothing. As my research had suggested, and as our local wanderings had shown us, Newbury One's battlefield is more or less lost.

Pete told the locals about our visit to the local playground.

'Ah, so you found our little piece of history, then, did you?'

'Yeah, little's the word, isn't it. Is that all that's left of the battlefield?' I interjected, taking full advantage of Pete's lead.

'No, no. The northern end of the battlefield's still farmland. You can still see it, but there are no monuments or markers that end. Nobody really has a clue where most of it happened. Don't suppose anyone ever will now.'

'Crazy, isn't it? Talking of monuments . . . you wouldn't happen to know why that monument out there is exclusively Royalist, would you? I've never see one so biased.'

'Ah, that's because it's not meant to be a Civil War monument, you see.'

I glanced out of the window at the huge Civil War monument across the road. Not meant to be a Civil War monument? What was it meant to be, then? A rocket, perhaps? If it wasn't meant to be a monument, then somebody had failed quite spectacularly during its construction.

'It's a Lord Falkland memorial,' the local continued, 'and as he was a Cavalier, they obviously decided to leave the Roundheads out of it.'

A Lord Falkland memorial. Yet another major historical site without a proper Civil War monument.

The anger rose within me. I counted to ten, composed myself, and resumed our conversation.

'Fair enough,' I said, thinking the exact opposite. 'But this area was pro-Parliament during the war – don't people round here feel a little resentful that a monument on their own doorstep should only represent the enemy?'

The local cut me a rather odd look and then, leaning conspiratorially towards me, said, 'This may come as a bit of a surprise to you, young man, but the war finished a few hundred years back now, and people round here, generally speaking, don't tend to rebel against the monarchy that much these days.'

A hail of peanuts flew into the air. If there's one thing Pete loves, it's me being made to look an idiot without his assistance. He was helpless, in fits of laughter. It was a horrible sight to behold. Every inch of the man vibrated and convulsed, his head seemed to expand to twice its normal size, spit and peanuts flowed copiously from his mouth and then, as a grisly finale, beer poured from his nostrils and splattered down his T-shirt.

The locals were as shocked as I was revolted. They couldn't seem to make their minds up whether Pete was laughing or dying. I held up a calming hand, probably preventing them from calling an ambulance.

'No, no,' I muttered, 'I take your point. I don't suppose there would be much concern nowadays.'

The local smiled, a little pityingly for my liking, and headed off to get Pete a towel.

As we left Wash Common, Newbury, and drove out to look at some nondescript farmland that was once a battlefield, Pete decided I'd had enough for one day, what with being hit by a car, misled by burial mounds, knocked flying by a Zimmer and ridiculed in a pub, and so, purely out of pity, he forced himself to discuss the Battle of Newbury with me.

'So, our Rupert – the nutter – he got beat for once then, did he?' slurred Pete.

'No, not at all. He was the Royalists' only winner on the day. He beat the Roundhead cavalry again. The Royalists couldn't break Parliament's lines, but Rupert won his own battle.'

'Unlike him to run off in the night, though. Must've hurt his feelings a bit.'

It must have indeed. Because while the rest of the Royalist army went on their way . . . Rupert and his cavalry lay in wait.

As soon as the jubilant Parliamentarians began making their way back to London, they received a vicious stab in the back. Rupert and his men rode into their rear, mounting a devastating, slashing raid on unprepared infantrymen that left many dead and wounded. His pride restored, Rupert rode back to the King, probably smiling innocently and claiming to have just nipped down the shops.

I have to admit though, for me, Newbury had been a huge disappointment, as well as a geriatric death trap. But the next venue on my diminishing list of major Civil War battles was the big one, the one I'd been looking forward to for months – Marston Moor, the largest battle ever fought on English soil.

And Marston Moor would leave nobody in doubt as to who'd won.

Marston Moor – The Toilet-Seat Offensive

In which the Author attempts to make small talk with the most violent man in Northern England

York is a lovely city. From the imposingly beautiful Minster and the ancient city walls, to the narrow, cobbled Shambles with its overhanging historic buildings and bustling streets full of little shops and restaurants, it is truly magnificent.

So why was it that Pete marched us straight into the only seedy-looking pub in town, empty but for a huge skinhead with 'England' tattooed across the back of his neck sitting at the bar, and an equally huge and far hairier individual behind it? The pub was silent but for the occasional skinhead grunt, barman cough and Pete slurp. I quickly finished my pint and got up to leave.

As proved at Chalgrove, Pete and I have extremely

different views on pubs, but how he could possibly have misconstrued my attempt to leave rapidly as an enthusiastic lurch for the bar, I don't know. Didn't he realise that there was an entire city full of decent pubs and bars just outside the door? How could he want to stay here? As if to emphasise my feelings about the place, Pete's shout of 'Pint of John Smith's please' became completely drowned out by a sudden and disturbingly loud gargling of saliva from the skinhead, along with a resultant projectile gob into a far corner of the room.

We'd been in York only twenty minutes, and this wasn't a brilliant reintroduction to a city I knew and loved. The reason we'd been in York only twenty minutes was also Pete's doing. As with our previous Yorkshire adventure, a planned early-morning Saturday start had ended with my breaking into Pete's house. This time it hadn't been a dog I'd found in the bedrooms – just nobody. Pete was nowhere to be found.

It was 11 a.m. before I finally heard from him. It turned out he'd 'pulled'. Pete had pulled. He hadn't pulled a woman in the last two years. Why did he have to pull one the night before our longest drive yet?

I eventually collected a very smug and happy Pete on his new friend's doorstep at one in the afternoon, and wiped the smile off his face as we pulled away by stating that Dave the dog had the edge on her. Which wasn't true at all. She was stunning. I was just so fed up at leaving SEVEN hours later than planned, there was no way I'd be paying anyone any compliments. Five minutes later, at the next set of lights, Pete got out of the car and walked away. Fifteen minutes kerb-crawling beside him and apologising for my comment couldn't repair the damage. He eventually vaulted a fence, nearly collapsing it, jogged down a side street and was gone. I pondered my next move. Our Mission had become a huge part of my entire write-up and story so far, and Pete was an integral part of it all. I realised I couldn't make the trip without him. Four phone calls to his mobile were ignored.

At that moment, it looked like the Mission was over.

Dejectedly, I turned the car around and started back home. As I pulled into my drive I wondered how I'd explain exactly why I'd called Pete's new girlfriend a dog, managed to screw up the day, lose my travelling companion and wreck our Mission.

I didn't have to. Before I could even reach my door, a taxi screeched round the corner and out jumped Pete. Before I could ask, Pete answered.

'Come on, then, let's go, we're on a mission from Lorraine, aren't we?!!'

With that he rushed up, apologised and bear-hugged me, taking every breath of air out of my body and nearly breaking my ribs. But the Mission was back on. I fell back into the car and we were away.

And so, a day mainly wasted (but not for Pete), we arrived in York at near-on seven o'clock, checked into our hotel and headed straight out to hit the town. Or at least, the worst pub in it.

'I thought we'd go down the road for one?' I said, fixing Pete with a stare and motioning towards the door.

'Why?' asked Pete, slightly taken aback. 'What's wrong with this place?'

The skinhead and barman turned to look at me. 'Yes, what is wrong with this place?' was the unspoken question.

'Nothing . . . it's just there's a lot of places to . . . '

'There's none like this place, though,' came an interruption from the direction of the bar.

I looked up, with no idea which of the two had spoken. Whoever it was, was certainly right on that point.

'Are you from London then, pal?' said the voice. I stared at the two men at the bar. Again, neither seemed to have moved a muscle. There was still absolutely no indication which one was speaking. The only clue was that the skinhead had his back to us, so unless the barman was a ventriloquist, it was odds-on I was chatting with the skinhead.

It didn't matter. I wasn't about to tell *anyone* I was from London. As a youngster, I'd thought it cool to pretend I was from the capital, rather than a small town thirty miles from it. I thought it made me seem street-wise, tough and cosmopolitan. It took me a long time to realise that this clever little ruse was the precise reason I so often got smacked in the mouth.

Whether through resentment or regional rivalries, there's a few people out there who seem to have a grudge against Londoners. You can pretty much tell which people might feel this way by their accent. If they sound like they're from the North, the Midlands, the West Country, East Anglia, the South Coast, Wales, Scotland or Ireland, there's every chance it's them. As a result, I tend not to say I'm from London any more. Which is fine, because I'm not.

'Yes,' replied Pete. 'We're from London . . . well, he is, anyway.'

The skinhead turned to stare at me; the barman frowned. The pub fell silent. Again.

Five minutes passed and then, 'On holiday?'

This time I'd been looking directly at the pair of them. The barman's lips definitely hadn't moved, so the question had to have come from the skinhead. Pete and I had just drained our glasses, so in the spirit of friendship I felt reigned – since I hadn't been beaten up for being a Londoner – I helpfully returned our empty glasses to the bar and answered his question directly.

Taking the detour round his backside and getting face side of him, I plonked the empties on the bar, and told him that we were here doing some book research and that we'd be going out to Marston Moor in the morning.

The skinhead's back stiffened. The barman looked tense. Slowly the skinhead's eyes rose to meet mine. They were swimming in his head. But they looked vaguely friendly. A smile played upon his lips, revealing a massive loss of teeth. He poked out a hand. A single finger protruded from his fist and pointed straight at me.

'Fuck off,' he ventured.

'Easy now, Colin,' said a slightly panicked barman.

The finger poked dangerously towards my right eye. 'Don't you bastard well talk to me, you fucking cheeky bastard.'

'Colin doesn't like people talking to him,' said the barman, worriedly edging back from the bar. I felt Colin had already explained that point quite well.

'COME ON, COLIN, LIGHTEN UP, THESE ARE FRIENDS OF MINE,' came a shout from behind me.

From behind me? I turned and looked. At the end of the bar, behind a barrel and almost completely obscured from view, sat a smartly dressed middle-aged man. So, this was who had been talking to us. Through this simple barrel-obstruction, I'd approached the biggest psychopath in the North of England and tried to tell him about my day.

The smartly dressed man's words had an instant soothing effect on Colin. His whole body seemed to slump back towards the bar. I nodded to the man in the suit, he nodded back. I turned around to Pete and stared at his empty chair. He'd gone. The rotten pillock had gone.

My mind was made up. He could walk the 300 miles home to Wycombe.

I stepped outside into the fresh spring evening air and looked up and down the street. He'd not only gone, but seemingly gone quite some way. Not a bloke you'd want alongside you in any war, it seemed. Out of the corner of my eye I noticed a fracas going on back in the pub I never wanted to visit again.

It is not often in life that you perform a full-blown, movie-style, jaw-dropping double take, but the view that confronted me demanded it.

Before me, playing out like a silent comedy through the window's murky glass, a suddenly reappeared Pete seemed to be dancing with the skinhead.

Well, not dancing with him exactly. More

dragging him backwards around the room by a toilet seat which was inexplicably wrapped around his neck. The smartly dressed man and the barman were desperately attempting to appease Pete from the wings, without getting physically involved. Not surprisingly. Here was a man who'd attacked Colin with a toilet seat. He was obviously insane.

I thought so too. I raced back into the pub and joined in the general cacophony of appeasement. The major stumbling block in negotiations for Colin's release appeared to be that Pete didn't want to let Colin go, mainly because Colin planned to kill him the moment he did so. For five full minutes we talked, a dance breaking out every thirty seconds as Colin attempted various escape manoeuvres and Pete employed evasive tactics (i.e. wrenching hard on his toilet seat).

Eventually agreement was reached. Colin would be locked in the toilet and Pete and I were to leg it. With one huge shove, barman, Smartly Dressed Man, lunatic-Pete and myself shoved both Colin and his stylish plastic necklace into the gents. The barman turned a key in the lock.

Pete and I raced off down the road, Pete drawing up breathless after only twenty yards and slipping into the next pub along.

I ran back the extra quarter-mile I'd covered to find Pete happily ordering pints.

'We can't stay in here! We're virtually next door to Colin.'

'Exactly. Last place he'd expect to find us.'

And Pete was right. That was the last we ever saw

of Colin. A little later in the evening, we sat in a fantastic pub in the heart of York. The Star Inn is one long pleasant lounge bar, with a collection of small and cosy oak-panelled rooms off its main stretch. The atmosphere was busy and fun, without being boisterous. It had been an hour since Pete's unexpected brawl, and for some reason, probably a sense of denial, I hadn't mentioned the subject at all. But now I was ready to find out exactly what had happened, and so made the mistake of enquiring. The answer was matter-of-fact, as if obvious.

'Saw you getting into trouble, decided I'd better nip in the gents for a quick leak – didn't want to get caught short in your ambulance. Then I noticed the bog seat wasn't attached, put two and two together, wrapped it round Colin's neck. As you do. That's it, really.'

As you do? I took a large swig of Bluebell Bitter and decided that maybe Pete was a bloke you'd want alongside you in a war after all.

And that's what we were here for. Not to start a new civil war of course (although we'd tried), but to visit the most famous site from the original.

Marston Moor. The best-known battle of them all. And not without reason. Marston Moor was a huge affair. Just eight miles from the city of York, out on a wide sweep of moorland, 45,000 men fought by far the largest and most decisive battle of the war to date.

In truth, the huge number of troops involved had little to do with the Royalists, whose numbers were only slightly greater than at Edgehill.

The Royalist leader on the day was Prince Rottweiler, or rather Prince Rupert, who'd been rewarded by Charles for his constant successes with outright command. Had I been one of Rupert's troopers during the Civil War, I'd have had very mixed feelings about it. I'd have noticed by this point that he was one of those blokes that would get me into a ruck anywhere, even in an empty field. A bit like Colin. I'd soon begin to question whether I wanted a life-and-death brawl every time my 18,000 mates and I went out for a walk. I'd also have to ask the question, 'Do I want a quiet day today, or all-out death and destruction? Hmm, I think I'd prefer to relax a little today . . . oh, sod it, Rupert's just fired a musket at that army over there. Here we go again.' On the other hand, I'd have been well aware I was with a winner. He *really* was someone I'd want alongside me in a war. After two years of undefeated combat, I'd have definitely felt a confidence bordering on invincibility.

And at Marston Moor, the Royalists needed to be invincible, for Parliament had upped the stakes somewhat. They were the reason for the huge numbers at Marston Moor, bringing 27,000 troops to the party.

The size of this army was the result of a large-scale Allied initiative. The still-peeved Scottish, under Lord Levin, had marched south to link up with Lords Fairfax and Manchester. Oliver Cromwell's Ironside cavalry were there, as was Sir Thomas Fairfax and his own cavalry. For Sir Thomas in particular, after his brave efforts at Adwalton, it must have been a very nice change to see the enemy so heavily outnumbered.

Outnumbered or not, Rupert was always going to fight. With 27,000 Parliamentarians and Scotsmen waiting for him, it'd have been rude not to.

Rupert's brief had been to take his men north and relieve the under-siege city of York. After taking stock of the situation (the situation being that the besieging enemy were out in the open on Marston Moor) he came up with a battle plan. It is hardly necessary for me to tell you what that plan might involve. The all-out attack was scheduled for dawn.

But then Rupert blundered. Upon taking an evening delivery of a warm and welcoming letter from the Earl of Newcastle, who was holed up with his soldiers within York's walls, Rupert replied with a surly note, reading something like, 'Yeah, yeah, whatever. Get your men out here first thing in the morning.'

If ever a man had to learn the 'importance of good manners' the hard way, it was Rupert at Marston Moor. Newcastle objected to the abrupt tone of Rupert's order. Both he and his military advisor, Lord Eythin, found Rupert's tone rude. They decided, therefore, that Rupert could stuff his early-morning start and that they'd be at the battle whenever they felt like it.

Militarily, their decision was disastrous. If Rupert had one thing in his favour, it had been the element of surprise. The Allies just didn't expect him to attack. With such a huge force assembled, who'd be mad enough to attack it? Rupert, obviously.

So sure were the Allies that an attack wasn't imminent, they'd actually begun withdrawing from Marston Moor. The entire Allied infantry had set off south in order to cut off Rupert's inevitable panicked flight. They really had no idea, did they?

By the time the remaining Allies realised that

Rupert didn't seem to have gone, and that he intended to fight them, a large number of their soldiers were quite a few hours' march away.

Urgent orders were sent to return immediately. The situation was critical, if Rupert attacked before they returned . . .

But Rupert couldn't attack. The offended Newcastle and Eythin made sure of it. Their soldiers were needed but were nowhere to be seen. Eventually, Newcastle and a small entourage of Yorkshire gentlemen arrived on the field. Lord Eythin and his men were busy, they told him, looting an abandoned Allied camp. They'd be along when they'd finished.

Rupert couldn't believe it. Here was the Allied army, in total disarray, their troops all over the place, and he didn't have the numbers available to attack them. He decided to attack anyway. But Newcastle argued, and eventually Rupert agreed that any attack would have to wait for Eythin. Rupert waited, and waited, and waited. Eythin finally arrived at four o'clock in the afternoon.

It was too late. The Allied army had returned in strength, and were deployed in full battle formation. They were completely ready and singing psalms. Rupert's task was now daunting to say the least. Facing him on Marston Moor was a huge army. On the right wing were 5,000 horse under Sir Thomas Fairfax, on the left a further 5,000 under Oliver Cromwell. In the centre stood the massed Allied infantry under Lords Levin, Manchester and Fairfax. Musketeers were interspersed at regular intervals among both cavalry and pikemen. This was an absolutely awesome force. Rupert still couldn't wait to attack it.

Eight miles and over 360 years away, Pete was attacking the biggest meal I'd ever seen. Food *and* fighting all in one night. The idea of a tapas bar is surely to order a little of a few dishes. When the waiter had asked, 'Tapas?' Pete's reply of 'Yes' had been blunt and unaccompanied by further information. This wasn't a mistake. He wanted all the tapas. Every dish and lots of it. And this pleased me immensely, for this was a hungry Pete rather than a thirsty one. A few pints in the Star had been enough to satisfy his beer-buds and now, merry rather than drunk, he was eating a troughful of food. There was every chance that, in the morning, he'd be fit enough to make an early start at the battlefield.

Two hours later, our hotel barman was running out of beer and begging Pete to go to bed.

It was 10.30 a.m. before we reached Marston Moor, finally arriving at the battlefield twenty-three hours later than originally intended. I felt I knew a little of Rupert's frustration at Eythin. But only a very little of it. Rupert had lost a decisive advantage. I'd just been annoyingly delayed by a travelling companion who'd suddenly taken on the persona of a yard-dog; shagging, fighting and eating his way through the last thirty-six hours.

And now, in keeping with his new identity, I left him in the car while I checked out Marston Moor. I suppose I could have let him out for a run, but I hadn't brought a carrier bag with me.

Marston Moor today is a huge sweep of country-side with an imposing roadside monument at its centre. Flanked by the villages of Tockwith to the west and Long

Marston off to the east, it's a lonely, wind-blown place. I say 'wind-blown' because of my own experience that day. I don't know if it's always windy. It's certainly open enough to be. But when I got out of the car, I was almost blasted off my feet. For a moment I thought I'd walked straight into an Edgehill-style ghostly re-enactment. The gale roared about me like cannon fire, I was swept across the road as if by a surge of charging men, and as I reached the monument and steadied myself, my glasses were blown ten feet ahead of me into the field.

Scrambling around like Velma from *Scooby-Doo*, able to see my glasses but needing four attempts to actually get hold of them, I glanced back towards the car to see Pete eyeing me with deep suspicion. You could feel and hear the wind in the car, but there was no real hint of the sheer force you felt the moment you stepped out into it. To Pete, my antics must have looked like those of a madman. Within seconds of closing the car door I'd suddenly run across a road, my whole body arching forwards, and then jumped around in a field and started scrambling in the dirt. No sooner had this thought crossed my mind than my notebook was blown to pieces. Literally blown to pieces. As if hit by an incoming musket ball, it just exploded in my hand. Paper flew everywhere, some of it twenty feet into the air, some of it halfway across Marston Moor.

I'd only made a few notes, so didn't even attempt to give chase. I glanced towards the car again, only to see Pete helpless with laughter. I fervently hoped that one particular piece of paper would land, letters facing inwards, on the windscreen directly in front of his eyes.

'PETE – TAPAS BAR/PIG. ALSO MENTION PETE'S LIKENESS TO YARD-DOG/ ANIMAL'. That would've wiped the grin off his face.

Finally regaining composure, I grabbed the camcorder from my coat pocket and began filming the monument and surrounding fields. This would have to be a visual record rather than a written one. Inspecting the monument closely I noted with great pleasure, far greater pleasure than should have been merited, that this monument was a *proper* one. It wasn't dedicated to any particular participant or local hero – it was a great big impressive monument commemorating the Battle of Marston Moor, the Civil War, and absolutely nothing else.

I filmed for a few minutes with a stupid grin on my face and then, out of the corner of my eye, I saw Pete climb from the car and lurch sideways in the wind. He was making for the hedge. He was going to take a leak behind a hedge. This was brilliant. Not only was he completely vindicating my yard-dog analogy, he was going to do something that no man in his right mind should ever do in a force-eight gale. I watched his head bobbing wildly behind the hedge for a few moments, sometimes lurching violently to the left, sometimes to the right, and then finally, to my absolute delight, he emerged looking seriously shaken and sporting an alarmingly large wet patch. And not just any old wet patch.

The wind had so aggressively disturbed Pete's unpleasant activities that the wet patch was not on his trousers but splattered half way up his T-shirt. Training my camcorder on him, I shouted a commentary over the roaring wind, 'This is Peter Ilic at the famous battlefield of Marston Moor. You will see he's just come out from behind a hedge, where he was attempting to take a leak in the middle of a hurricane. Please note if you will, the huge wet stain on the front of his T-shirt. Ladies and gentlemen of the Prince of Wales [for this was where I planned to screen it], this is a rarely seen event. This man has pissed his shirt!'

Just to add to my entertainment, and to provide a slightly disturbing encore, Pete stumbled to the boot of the car, ripped off his T-shirt, and stood wobbling and vibrating in the wind. It was as if unseen hands had taken hold of his belly and decided to give it a violently enthusiastic shaking. He finally dragged a new shirt from his holdall and re-dressed. That last scene made my recording a 'video-nasty'. I decided that no person of tender years or squeamish nature should ever see this footage.

Turning my attention back to the job in hand, I struggled over to an information board showing the two armies' deployment. It explained that I was standing between the two armies, ahead of me to the north were the Royalists, and behind me to the south, the Allies. The Royalists had deployed in much the same traditional manner as their enemies, with 10,000 infantrymen in the centre and almost 5,000 horse on the wings, supported by 500 musketeers on the left. A ditch ran between the two armies, and Rupert deployed further musketeers along its length, hoping that the combination of ditch and musket fire would disrupt any Allied advance. Around 700 horse were kept in reserve.

As my mind is wont to do, it began wandering.

The gales blowing me back and forth faded into insignif-icance, the sky darkened with storm clouds, the monument, road and car disappeared. I stood on Marston Moor on 2 July 1644.

In the field ahead of me, there was nothing but frustration for Prince Rupert. His intentions of an early attack already thwarted, he was now struggling with Eythin's and Newcastle's open criticism of his deploy-ment and plans. Eythin complained that they had moved too close to the Allied lines, while both Eythin and Newcastle disagreed with his eagerness to attack, and suggested they wait until morning.

Rupert was thoroughly fed up. His first planned attack had been rendered impossible by the late arrival of his comrades, his second was now a matter of hostile debate. The day had been a waste of time. It was early evening and hardly anyone was dead.

What Rupert did next is a measure of his mood. He did something totally alien to him. He decided to eat rather than fight. Reasoning that it was probably too late in the day to start a battle anyway, and so hardly worth the bickering, he allowed his troops to break rank and eat while he rode dejectedly to the rear. The battle really would have to wait until the morning.

The atmosphere had thickened dramatically over the last hour or so and a huge storm looked to be on the way. It certainly was. At 7.30 p.m., a massive clap of thunder roared above the open moor. Ferocious rain poured down. Suddenly the entire Allied front line surged across the field.

I stared to the south. What a terrifying sight it

must have been. Through the lashing rain, the Royalists would have strained to see what was happening. In fact, 11,000 infantry and 10,000 cavalry were coming straight at them. The Royalists desperately scrambled themselves into fighting order. But the armies' close deployment meant that the Allies were virtually upon them.

Cromwell and his Ironsides charged through the rain into the Royalist right flank, meeting a hastily organised cavalry counter-attack at the ditch. But the Royalist cavalry were blocking the view of their own musketeers, who could do nothing to assist. Cromwell's men slammed into their opponents, completely routing the Royalist horse. An alarmed Rupert rode forward from the rear, reorganised his retreating cavalry and led a second counter-charge.

But the Ironsides would not be halted. And as they cut into the Royalists once more, they were supported by a Scottish cavalry flank attack. Rupert's cavalry were hit from all sides. As Rupert's own Lifeguard Troops fought for their lives around him, he himself was unseated from his horse.

Rupert's cavalry were destroyed. The entire Royalist right wing was smashed. The Allies were running rampage. Somehow, Rupert scrambled from the carnage and into a crop field, where he hid to avoid being captured. What else could he do?

Meanwhile, as part of this huge co-ordinated attack, the Allied infantry rushed headlong into the Royalist centre and Sir Thomas Fairfax's cavalry charged at the Royalist left wing. The Royalists had been hit hard and fast in every area of the field.

And then, things started going dramatically wrong for the Allies.

As Sir Thomas's cavalry arrived at the long ditch, Rupert's defensively deployed musketeers opened fire. The Allied cavalry tried desperately to cross the ditch under heavy fire, but casualties began to mount. As they attempted to pull back in disarray, the left-wing Royalist cavalry charged forward. Fairfax's cavalry was smashed.

The Royalist's right-flank disaster had been countered by an Allied disaster on theirs. Indeed, mirroring Rupert, Sir Thomas found himself desperately needing to take flight. Completely cut off from his men by marauding Royalists, he ripped off his officer's insignia and galloped away to meet up with Cromwell.

With their opposing cavalry shattered and retreating, the left wing Royalist cavalry immediately turned their attention to the centre of the field.

With a resolute and unbroken Royalist line providing tough opposition, the Allied infantry had enough on their plate. The last thing they needed was a sudden onslaught by horsemen.

The Allied centre virtually disintegrated. The panic was so great that, despite knowing the deadly risk of breaking ranks, a number of entire regiments turned and fled. The 27,000-strong Allied army was collapsing.

And so was my all-too-brief fantasy. From the south, my disgruntled dog was effecting his own charge across Marston Moor. It was lunchtime.

We decided that Tockwith, with the Boot and Shoe and the Spotted Ox to choose from, would be ideal.

After a brief game of eeny-meeny-miney-mo, we stepped through the door of the Boot and Shoe and knew we'd made the right choice. Not only was it a perfect little pub, oak-beamed with a coal fire and brick bar, it had Civil War memorabilia aplenty. Hanging on the walls were brass Cavalier face plaques, battle flags, pikes, helmets, body armour and battle maps. In a glass case that resembled a fish tank, a die-cast miniature re-enactment of the battle was taking place. It was by far the best display I'd seen since the Castle Inn at Edgehill. And this was just the lounge bar. There was still the snug bar and pool room to go. These turned out to commemorate World War Two, rather than the Civil War; the walls were covered in prints of military aircraft and battleships.

There was more joy to come, though. Two pints of Samuel Smith's Sovereign bitter cost only £2.40. Two pounds forty! Two pints would have cost more than double that anywhere else. I actually checked if the barman had made a mistake. No. Unbelievable. Both Pete and I were deliriously happy; he with the price of a pint, me because I was totally surrounded by Civil War curiosities.

The ridiculously low-priced food added even more to the experience. Pete was served up a whale on a plate with a bucketful of chips, while I settled for a baguette which turned out to be the best part of a French loaf.

And, as we ate, the conversation at the bar proved to be unforgettable. Delivered in the barman's Geordie-sounding accent along with the locals' Yorkshire brogue, it was sheer comedy.

'You know that lad who was on *Stars In Their Eyes?*'

'Aye . . . er . . . no.'

'The one that did Freddie Mercury a long while back?'

'How do you mean?'

'On *Stars In Their Eyes.*'

'Oh, aye. No.'

'Well, his mum drinks in here.'

'Really?'

'Aye. I never knew that was his mum.'

'No.'

'But he was in with her the other day.'

'Oh, aye.'

'And do you know what he said?'

'No.'

'He said, "Matthew Kelly put me at ease".'

'Really?'

'Aye. I've always wanted to hear someone say that. "Matthew Kelly put me at ease". Brilliant.'

'Aye.'

And so it went on. Pete and I munched our meals without ever taking our eyes off the group at the bar. It was as if they'd put a cabaret on for us. Their humour was easy-going and finely tuned. It was a pleasure to listen to them. And just as much of a pleasure to drink beer at half-price. Pete got through a further two pints, one of Samuel Smith Cask ale, the other of Samuel Smith Stout. It was then a simple matter of crossing the street to nip into the Spotted Ox for a pint. While almost worth a very brief visit, it was a mainly football-orientated pub. Flags and TV screens adorned its walls, and wall-to-wall blokes struggled to speak to each other over the general hubbub of music and noise. It was popular and packed, and there was a varied selection of decent ales on offer, including Timothy Taylor Landlord, one of my all-time favourite beers and, somewhat surprisingly, described by world superstar Madonna (whom I just can't imagine supping a pint) as the 'champagne of ales'.

But I wasn't allowed any more drinks, one being my limit when driving. And there was no Civil War memorabilia. They'd left that to the Boot and Shoe. Pete enjoyed a brief argument at the bar regarding football, the gist of it being that he didn't approve, and then we were on our way to Long Marston. The Tockwith to Long Marston road passes through the battlefield, and so I automatically stopped for another bout of staring, trying hard to once again capture the atmosphere of that dramatic encounter. Pete's constant tutting became aggravating, so I stepped from the car and, as the wind roared like cannon once more, 1644 came flooding back.

A huge Allied army on the brink of disaster. The Royalist cavalry and infantry ploughing into a courageous but dangerously unprotected Allied centre.

But help was approaching fast. The Ironsides and their Scottish allies had raced around the battlefield and now charged into the Royalist left wing. The surprised Royalist cavalry were hit hard, driven back, and out of the fight.

For the second time in the evening, Cromwell and company had routed their Royalist counterparts. Suddenly the battle had a whole new look to it. Now it was the Royalist infantry who were unprotected and facing the deadly combination of a joint infantry and cavalry attack. And with both wings of their cavalry defeated, there was no hope of rescue.

The Royalist infantry fought hard, but it was over. Newcastle's own regiment, the Whitecoats, fought incredibly bravely, battling on and on against repeated Ironside charges. They wouldn't surrender and fought until all but twenty to thirty of an original 3,000 men were killed.

Cromwell had led his cavalry across all areas of the field, and defeated the Royalist right, left and centre. For the first time in the war, Prince Rupert's cavalry had been beaten. Over 4,000 Royalists lay dead, and many more were prisoners. The field had been totally won. The Royalists had not only lost the battle, but were forced to leave behind their ammunition, gunpowder, supplies and baggage. The North now belonged to Parliament and their Allies. Marston Moor had been a Royalist disaster.

Climbing back into the car to the sound of further tuts of disapproval, I drove the short distance to Long Marston and the battlefield's third pub.

The Sun Inn is a very long, very narrow pub, consisting of one room cut into four sections, with a further small snug bar to the rear. It's another black-beamed, pleasant pub, serving exactly the same choice of beers as the Boot and Shoe in Tockwith: Samuel Smith's Sovereign, Cask and Stout. There was plenty more Civil War memorabilia here too, making it an impressive two pubs out of three at Marston Moor.

Prince Rupert's portrait hung among those of his

enemies – General Alexander Leslie, Oliver Cromwell, the Earl of Manchester, Sir Thomas Fairfax. A helmet and battle map completed the collection.

One section of the pub was packed with a lively bunch of elderly men who all sounded exactly like Johnny Vegas. Seeing as Johnny Vegas is a Lancastrian and we were in North Yorkshire, this only goes to show how untrained my southern ears are. We sat at a table close to them, me filling up with Diet Coke, Pete slurping happily on stout. 'Slurp' was the word. He seemed to be trying to suck the liquid from its glass. Or perhaps he was lapping at it . . . like a yard-dog. Either way, after a few minutes of this unsavoury, gargling performance, he offered me a sip because it was 'delicious'. I tried to decline but found I had no choice, the glass being thrust so forcefully to my mouth that beer slopped into my eyes.

Despite my only view being a face full of stout, it was actually another beer that caught my attention. A lager, in fact, and lagers rarely catch my attention. Lagers are just something I usually tolerate when abroad or in a heat wave. But this lager was worthy of attention simply for being a totally obscure brand and yet available in two out of the three pubs we'd visited. I'd noticed Ayingerbrau lager in the Boot and Shoe, mainly because its bar-tap picture of a happily beaming moustachioed old boy in Bavarian dress had looked suspiciously like the old regular sitting next to it. And now here it was again, the same lager I'd never heard of, and the same old boy beaming happily at me from the pump. Odd.

What was this beer? Was the picture really of the

old boy in the Boot and Shoe? Did he perhaps brew the beer in his shed? In Bavaria? Or Tockwith? I asked one of the Johnny Vegas delegation.

'Whoever it is you think looks like that,' rasped Vegas, pointing at the bar-tap Bavarian, 'don't go telling him! He's called the Ayingerbrau Fatman.'

I realised that this was indeed good advice. Pointing at a stranger in a pub and suggesting he was the spitting image of the 'Ayingerbrau Fatman' was only likely to get me either soaked in beer or involved in another toilet-seat episode.

'It's a Sam Smith's beer, is that,' rasped another Johnny Vegas.

'Aye, Sam Smith's, is that,' rasped another.

There was a general nodding of heads. It was a Sam Smith's beer. Which made sense. I'd been in two Samuel Smith's pubs and both served Ayingerbrau. You didn't have to be a genius, but you did have to have a little more deductive reasoning than I was exhibiting. What can you expect from a man who sways in force-eight gales pretending it's 1644?

We had a long chat with the locals. Here at last was a battlefield that people knew about and visited. Lots of tourists came to Marston Moor. For the first time on our travels thus far, we'd come to a Civil War battlefield that people still had an interest in. Adwalton Moor may be largely forgotten, and the Rye totally forgotten – even Edgehill seemed rather neglected, if only by the majority of its local pubs. But not Marston Moor. The Battle of Marston Moor may be over 360 years old, but it's still alive and well.

Pete didn't give a toss. He wouldn't hear talk of an Ayingerbrau Fatman without drinking his lager. By three o'clock, the Ayingerbrau Fatman had a new friend, and the Wycombe Fatman had loads of new friends, all of them Johnny Vegas.

At three-thirty, as far as Pete was concerned, it was time for 'lights out'. We were by now speeding south, and the usual grunts that precede full-blown grating snores were just starting. Pete had had only fifteen conscious minutes in which to astound and annoy me on the journey home, but succeeded nevertheless. Moments before passing out, he'd yawned and muttered, 'So . . . the Royalists won again, did they? It's a wonder Parliament ever won that war.'

'What? No! It was a . . . '

I realised my travelling 'companion' was now asleep. How could he have spent two days in Yorkshire, listening to me rave on about the battle at every opportunity, visiting the battlefield and looking at pub battle maps, without having any idea whatsoever what had happened?

'. . . major Royalist defeat,' I finished, my voice fading to silence.

It certainly had been major. But the Royalists weren't finished yet. The North had been lost and Rupert defeated, but it wasn't over. A large Royalist army still remained to the south with Charles. Meanwhile Rupert rebuilt and recruited. There was plenty of fight in the Royalists yet. But a fight was certainly what they were going to get. The new Parliamentarian army had become strong and well organised. Cromwell,

Fairfax and Manchester epitomised its steely resolve. They were now a force to be reckoned with.

It was after eight in the evening when I arrived home in Wycombe. I threw my camcorder and notes onto the desk and decided I'd write them up in the morning. But, before giving in to my six-year-old daughter's arm tugs and gleeful requests for me to 'come and see what I've done to the cat', I quickly typed 'York – skinhead – Colin-attack-toilet-seat' as Internet keywords. Fortunately there was no relevant news on the subject but there were some interesting results nevertheless, including an incident involving a woman 'attached' to a high-pressure vacuum toilet. A skinhead was nearby.

I also typed in 'Ayingerbrau'. It would seem that Ayingerbrau isn't obscure after all. It would appear, in fact, to be just about everywhere. It's about as common a draught lager as we have in this country. I spend all this time in pubs, probably staring at an Ayingerbrau pump at least once a week . . . and I've never, ever noticed.

With my acute observational skills, it's little wonder I became a writer.

The Twilight Zone

*In which the Author finds absolutely nothing in a field
. . . and is terrified by it*

Chalgrove Field, on a dull May afternoon.

I walked from my car to the area my extensive research had clearly identified as that spooky area where no animals run and no birds fly. Well, extensive in that I asked lots and lots of people, but nobody could confirm the story I'd heard in the Lamb pub.

Not until I mentioned the subject at a family get-together and my uncle's ears pricked up (he's very catlike). He'd lived in Chalgrove in the 1970s and knew all about the 'deserted bit', as he called it. He also knew exactly whereabouts it was, and happily marked the spot on my OS map. (I would like to point out that he marked the spot a few days later. I don't turn up at parties clutching OS maps. Not very often, anyway.)

Reaching a narrow copse of trees between two

fields, I checked my map, checked the trees, checked my map . . . this was it.

I sat down on my outspread coat and studied this small dark clump of woodland. Scanning the trees ahead for signs of life, I began to feel incredibly woozy. I realised I was holding my breath. Subconscious anticipation, I think. I desperately didn't want to see a bird or a squirrel in those tree tops. I wanted this nonsense to be real. A touch of the unexplainable always gives me a tingle. Since my late vigil at Edgehill, I'd made a point of checking out related ghost stories after every battlefield visit. Most offered little, and what they did offer sounded dodgy and unlikely at best, but my most recent battlefield – Marston Moor – turned out to have a more than healthy share of sightings and peculiarities to its name.

Marston Moor-related hauntings started on the very night of the Royalist's hammering, when the Earl of Newcastle's heroic Whitecoats rode back to their head-quarters at Bolsover Castle, the Earl's fortified stately home.

At Marston Moor, of course, the Whitecoats took the severest casualties the war had yet seen, and the very few who didn't die on the field were captured.

So who rode into Bolsover Castle?

Who were the horsemen who rode into Bolsover's stables? Who were the soldiers who arrived with much clattering and clanking of steel? It couldn't have been the Whitecoats, because they were dead. Apparently, it was.

Old habits die hard, and for soldiers who'd died as hard as the Whitecoats, even harder it would seem.

Just as they had after all previous battles, outings, skirmishes and sieges, the Whitecoats returned noisily to Bolsover Castle to bed down for the night.

The residents of the castle clearly heard them going about their evening business, heard their banter and shouts, but there was nobody there. No horses, no soldiers, no survivors.

Nothing but empty gardens, statues and shadows.

Thus started the haunting of Bolsover Castle, and it continues to this day. Groups of Civil War soldiers, presumably the very same Whitecoats, are heard marching around the castle grounds in the dead of night. Occasionally, they have even been seen, parading against a backdrop of mist and moonlight.

And it would appear that their boss, the Earl himself, is also still in residence. I read a report stating that he likes to kick female guides at the castle. And why would he want to do that? Apparently because he was a notorious womaniser, and the report goes on to suggest that he kicks them for 'revenge'. This does not seem a satisfactory explanation. What thought processes went into that one? 'Well, during his life he loved women, you see, and he had a brilliant time with them, and they made him very, very happy . . . so now he kicks them . . . for revenge.'

Sounds to me that if anybody's kicking females at Bolsover, it's surely the Earl's wife.

I've since read an alternative piece claiming that women at the castle often claim to have had their backsides pinched and slapped by an invisible hand. Now, that sounds more like the Earl's work.

Another famous Bolsover ghost is that of another Civil War soldier; this one within the castle walls. A guide, while waiting for a group of tourists, ironically whom he was about to take on a 'ghost tour' of the castle, suddenly saw the flickering image of a Cavalier, in full period clothing, walk across the room and disappear through a wall. It's not recorded how the ghost tour went, but we can rest assured that the guide would have taken his work quite seriously from then on.

I spent quite some time scouring library and Internet records for reported hauntings connected with Marston Moor, and the thing I found most remarkable was the consistency of people's stories. Three particular ghostly Cavaliers crop up continually throughout history.

Mention of these spectres dates way back into the dim distant past, to not many years after the battle in fact, and during the intervening centuries sightings have not diminished. In fact, they've become more frequent with the passage of time, which may of course be attributable to the fact that more people pass through the area these days, and so while the ghosts have always been there, the observers have not.

Modern-day walkers have often seen the ghostly threesome way out on the moor, and drivers along its lonely roads regularly report seeing three soldiers in Civil War dress, clambering from a ditch at the side of the road. Could it be one of the very same ditches used to defend against cavalry charges during the battle? Many died horribly in those ditches. Are some still climbing from their place of death, all these years on?

So real do the soldiers look, that many witnesses

initially believe them to be normal flesh-and-blood men in fancy dress. One particular motorist, straining to see from around a quarter of a mile off, observed the ghosts' customary climb from their ditch. By the time he drew closer, they were standing in the middle of the road. He pulled to a halt to let them cross. They didn't look like phantoms. He was convinced they were real, solid human beings. But, as he drove on and looked in his mirror, he was surprised to see that the road behind him was completely empty. There was no one to be seen for miles.

So stunned was he that he reversed to the spot, got out and looked around. Nothing. An empty ditch and empty fields. They'd vanished into thin air.

So why, I've often wondered, are so many Civil War soldiers apparently still walking the earth today?

I've heard one paranormal expert state that many hauntings are carried out by people 'who died suddenly and violently, didn't expect to die, and so have never accepted that they are dead'.

This may or may not be so, but can this theory really apply to Civil War soldiers? Sure, they died suddenly and extremely violently . . . but they didn't *expect* it? Standing in a field, faced with a charging mass of sharp-edged swords, lethal pikes and galloping horses, they didn't expect to die? If they truly didn't, then these people's names should appear in the Oxford English Dictionary under the word 'optimistic'.

As for them not accepting they're dead, that seems a little petulant to me. If your head's been lopped off by a Roundhead sword and is rolling away under a horse's hooves, I'd think that you'd pretty much have to accept that you were, almost definitely, dead.

My own theory is based on the percentages game. If thousands of people come to horrible ends in a meadow on the same day, I feel that, by the law of percentages, that meadow is thousands of times more likely to be haunted than a meadow that's seen one death in the last five hundred years – say by a drunken man attempting to ride a cow, breaking his neck.

A drunken man attempting to ride a cow isn't an 'off the top of the head' example, by the way. No, late-night inebriated cow-riding is yet another example of Pete's colourful dabblings in the dangerous world of farmyard animals. Sadly, Pete wasn't killed though. Instead, he ended up rolling into a cowpat, where he eventually got a good night's sleep, only to be awoken at dawn by the cow urinating on his face. Some things are worse than dying.

Anyway, taking this 'percentages' idea one last step – of the many, many thousands that died during these battles, there must have been at least one or two individuals, that warped 0.5 per cent, who, in keeping with our aforementioned paranormal expert's theory, truly believed that:

a) no harm could possibly come to them, and
b) despite the lack of any functioning organs whatsoever, they weren't dead.

So there you have it . . . solved. Ghosts are idiots.

But back to reality – or a slight lack of it, because here I was sitting in a field, staring at a copse and hoping for nothing to happen. Nothing happening would prove something was happening here.

And so I sat for hours. A squirrel sat with me for a while, and a few birds nipped down to share my sandwiches, but not once did I see any movement whatsoever in the clump of trees ahead. At regular intervals I scanned the tree tops with binoculars for signs of life (getting quite a picture here, aren't we – a man sitting alongside a squirrel in a damp field, staring at nothing in particular through a pair of binoculars; never approach anybody like that). Not only did no birds fly over the area, many changed direction in midair seemingly to actively avoid it.

After a while, I became entirely satisfied that the area was indeed devoid of mammalian and bird life. I decided it was time to experiment by placing a mammal in there and seeing what happened. Being a mammal, I nominated myself.

I stood and walked tentatively towards the copse. Tentatively because, for some reason, probably because of the legends surrounding it, those trees looked extremely foreboding.

I'm sure this was all in my head, but the nearer I got, the more I wanted to turn and leave. A feeling of stress seemed to overtake me. I could hear my own heartbeat in my ears, and my hands became sweaty. I reached the first tree. I clenched my fists in anticipation, stepped forward, and immediately jumped out of my skin.

It was my car horn. Its sudden loud honking gave me the shock of my life. 'Wait a minute, you fat git,' I thought, 'can't you see I'm busy?' I turned to the trees again, my horn honked again, and again and again.

What was the matter with this bloke? Wait, you moron. I stared at the hedge beside which my car was parked. The honking suddenly stopped. What did the idiot want? Suddenly, I wondered if something was wrong. Surely he'd have got out of the car by now. Was he having a heart attack or something, and honking for help? Was I ignoring Pete honking for heart help?

I ran full pelt across the field, got halfway and stopped dead.

There was no way Pete was honking that horn. Because Pete wasn't with me today. I can be a little misty-minded at the best of times, but I think my distraction at the copse had clouded me completely. The moment I'd heard that horn, I thought 'Pete'. But nobody was in my car. I was on my own.

I walked to the hedge, ducked though a gap in its foliage and came face to face with my car. It sat alone in a country lane, looking peaceful and innocent, and seeming to say, 'Who, me? I didn't beep.'

I looked up and down the lane. No other cars around. I was sure the beeping came from my car, but my car has no alarm system, and has never been prone to honking on its own before. I climbed inside and switched on the ignition. Everything seemed normal. This was a shrug-and-forget-it moment. I shrugged and forgot it.

Five minutes later I was again approaching the dreaded copse. Now I was really edgy. My heart hadn't calmed down from the (forgotten) horn business. I reached the trees. I stepped forward. I heard a shout from somewhere behind me. I turned and stared across the empty field. Nothing. Nobody. My horn beeped.

This was ridiculous. For the first time in my life I seriously felt that I was experiencing something paranormal. My horn beeped again. I could feel myself shaking.

I ignored the horn and stepped towards the trees. I heard a shout, and my horn beeped continuously. I glanced over my shoulder but continued walking . . . straight between the trees and into the darkened copse.

I think that my whole set of experiences thus far would have very much contributed to my state of mind at that moment, but I have to say I felt a chill and a terror run through me that virtually paralysed my arms and legs. It was an effort of will to simply turn my head and look around me. I could hear nothing but my own heartbeat, and my inclination was to turn and run as fast as I could – which wouldn't be very fast at all, considering my legs were frozen.

Calm down, I thought, breathe, yes, that's it, breathe, because you're not breathing again and you're about to collapse.

Not only did I manage to breathe, I began exercising a breathing technique taught to me recently, which involves imagining yourself surfing on your own belly, and riding the breaths in and out, in and out, like the tides, in and out. My body relaxed, my terror subsided. I was standing in a patch of trees in a field in broad daylight. I walked around and studied branches, bushes and leaves. There were insects here, and the insects didn't look worried. But then they had nothing to worry about, because there was clearly nothing else around. Just me, and the insects.

I stayed for about an hour, sometimes scouting around, occasionally standing very still so as not to scare away any approaching wildlife that could refute this old story.

I heard no more shouts and my horn remained silent. Eventually, I walked back to my car and headed for home. Throughout the course of an entire afternoon, I had seen not one animal, other than ants and bugs, in among those trees.

The beeps and shouts were odd, but rationality tells me the sounds may well have carried from elsewhere. My conclusion, though, is that Chalgrove Field's dead zone is real, and a very strange phenomenon indeed. Probably.

Around two hours later I realised I'd left my coat in the middle of the field. I've never seen it since.

Death on the Fairway – The Second Battle of Newbury

In which the Author attempts to book a table for 20,000 while Pillock shoots himself in the head

Some places are worth visiting twice. While I personally have never attributed this particular phrase to Newbury, Berkshire, the armies of King and Parliament did.

Pete's views, for once, were rather closer to mine.

'Why the fuck are we going to Newbury again?'

'I told you. There were two Battles of Newbury.'

'That's not an answer.'

As it quite clearly was an answer, I waited for Pete to elaborate.

'What I don't understand is why we have to go there twice?'

'Because . . . '

'Don't give me that old "two battles" rubbish again.'

This was going nowhere. I parked up at the Hare and Hounds Hotel Bar and Restaurant in the picturesque village of Speen, near Newbury, and looked my companion square in the face.

'What do you want me to tell you, Pete?'

'Tell me why.'

I held my stare.

'Why twice? Why didn't you do both battles the first time we came here? Seems stupid driving all the way out here twice.'

'Oh, I see what you mean. I want to do all the battles chronologically, so I sort of get a feeling of travelling through the war. You didn't moan about going to Yorkshire twice and that's a bloody sight further than Newbury.'

Pete's face suddenly darkened. Something was very wrong. His brows furrowed and his jaw hardened, giving one a glimpse of something buried deep in our primeval history.

'We – went – to – Yorkshire . . . TWICE?? Are you kidding me?'

'You know we did.'

'No I bloody – Hang on . . . are you telling me Adwalton's in Yorkshire?'

Mine and Pete's early career in the courier and transport trade mean that obviously neither of us have the beginnings of a clue geographically, but even I was stunned that he didn't know he'd been to Yorkshire twice.

'Where did you think it was?'

'Near Leeds.'

'That's right . . . in Yorkshire.'

Pete's face turned a deathly shade of white. He suddenly leaped from the car and strode towards the Hare and Hounds, kicking pebbles violently into the air. Had he been hunched, wearing skins and carrying a stone club, he would have looked the full part.

I'd seriously annoyed him, I knew. He hates travelling even short distances. He really couldn't believe I'd dragged him to the same distant area twice. He had a point. Maybe I should have visited the two battlefields at once. It would have saved an awful lot of time and money. But I really did want to do this war properly, and if that meant Pete suffering, that was fine by me.

As with most of Pete's moods, his latest diminished upon reaching a bar. And the Hare and Hounds was definitely one to lift the spirits.

Decorated without a hint of Civil War recognition, but with plenty of charming landscapes, county maps, leather-bound mirrors, black-beamed ceilings and with an impressive array of beers including London Pride, Butts Traditional and Charles Wells Bombardier, it was a great place to start the day. But we weren't here for the beer. Not at this time of day. I quite clearly remember thinking this as Pete plonked two pints of Butts on the table.

'No way,' I protested, 'I'm not drinking at ten-thirty in the morning.'

'Don't worry, your girly coffee's on the way. The pint's for Dave.'

At this point, we both realised something was missing. It was Dave.

'Is he . . . ?' started Pete.

'. . . still in the car? He must be. Did he get in?'

The worrying thing was that neither of us were sure. Pete and I surely represent one of history's finest coming together of minds. We'd travelled an hour on the motorway, and had no idea whatsoever whether the man accompanying us was actually with us. I certainly remembered him standing outside Pete's gate at 9 a.m., but knowing whether he'd managed to get in the back seat before I pulled away was beyond me. If he had, he'd been very quiet.

My coffee arrived as Pete took my keys and hurried off to check the car for life-signs. Dave had been looking forward to this trip. This was the very same Dave who'd put us up in Leeds, and Pete was returning the compliment for a few nights – Dave using Pete's spare room as a base while visiting his very overcrowded brother's. Little did he know that he was sleeping in a bed last occupied by his own dog. I'd noticed Dave had been scratching rather a lot since his arrival – not surprising really, as the concept of changing bedclothes is quite alien to Pete.

Happily, a few minutes later a bleary-eyed Dave stumbled behind Pete into the bar.

'Curra chuffin' wokusup,' grumbled Dave.

Pete and I glanced at one another. A slight problem we'd had in Yorkshire was rearing its ugly head once more, namely that we could rarely understand a word Dave said. We'd been OK on his territory, because his wife had translated, but here in the South he was on his own with a foreign language. Well, not foreign exactly, but an incredibly fast, muttering form of deep Yorkshire dialect that generally left us stumped.

I'd got the gist of his first sentence though, and we certainly would have woken him, had we any recollection of him being with us.

Pete and Dave happily supped a couple of pints each while I studied a table full of OS maps, battle maps and texts. As usual my careful calculations led me to the bar to ask where on earth the battlefield was.

I stood waiting for a couple of minutes, but the place seemed suddenly deserted. Then I heard a voice, incredibly like that of John Cleese's Basil Fawlty from the 1970s sitcom *Fawlty Towers*, echoing from the kitchens:

'Look, I get very, very stressed, very, very quickly, all right? All right?'

I don't know who he'd addressed this remark to, but he was then suddenly in front of me.

He was *uncannily* Fawlty-like. His face was nothing like the original, but there was something in his whole demeanour that cried out Cleese. He was tall, gangly, red in the face, well dressed without looking in the slightest bit smart, and very, very stressed. And I knew he'd got this way very quickly.

He looked at me and I just knew he wanted to shriek, 'WELL? YES? WHAT IS IT? CAN'T YOU SEE I'M BUSY?'

Instead, he made a visible attempt to calm himself and went for plan B.

'We're closed, I'm afraid. We open at twelve.'

'Closed?' I said, glancing back at our table full of drinks. 'We've been here half an hour, we've already been served.'

Basil craned his neck around me and glanced at our table.

'Well, I'm afraid you shouldn't have been. Never mind. Can't be helped now.'

'Eh, OK. I wonder if you have any idea where the battlefield is around here?'

'The battlefield?'

'The Battle of Newbury? Second battle. A lot of it happened around this village. Any idea where?'

'Here? In Speen? What battle's this? Second World War?'

Out of the corner of my eye I saw Pete waving frantically at me, beckoning me to return to the table. I asked to be excused for one moment and went to see what the problem was.

Pete had obviously noted the Basil Fawlty likeness. Pulling me close and whispering in my ear, he rasped, 'Don't mention the war . . . I mentioned it once, but I think I got away with it!'

I tutted impatiently and strode back to the bar, where Basil was consulting his young assistant, who apparently shouldn't have served us. The assistant, who we shall call Polly for want of a better name, did indeed know of a local World War Two battle, but couldn't remember anything about it. No shame in that – 60 million other Britons would have to admit they couldn't remember much about the German army pushing as far west as Berkshire.

'It was actually a Civil War battle. A lot of it took place on Speen Heath.'

'Ah, Speen Heath. Down the lane opposite. Most of it's a golf club now, though.'

I thanked the cast and rallied Pete and Dave. We were very near our first target.

'Wherawa goan in sucha 'urry, ivenot dunwisuppinmebrew ye'twat.'

I looked at Pete; Pete looked at me.

'Yes,' I replied.

Five minutes later we somehow completely missed Speen Heath and drove into Donnington Castle's car park. This was fine, though. Donnington Castle would be as good a starting place as any. I climbed the steep hill to the castle ruins, with Dave a few yards behind me, and Pete way back, only ten paces up the hill in fact, red in the face and almost on his knees with exhaustion.

The view was stunning. The fields stretched out all around me, as they had for Royalist artillerymen on the day of the battle. It was hugely refreshing to find a battlefield that retained something as substantial as a castle – something that had actually been involved in the fighting all those centuries ago. These castle ruins saw a huge battle raging in the fields below, during which its occupants poured artillery fire down onto any Parliamentarian divisions that came within range.

Newbury Two was an odd sort of battle. It came a year and a month after the bloody fight on nearby Wash Common, and this time the action centred around an area to the north of town, a few miles from the original battle site. What was odd was that it was quite literally all over the place. The Royalists held the aforementioned fortified positions at Donnington Castle, and also at Shaw House, a few miles away, while the main bulk of the 9,000-strong army occupied entirely defensive positions on Speen Heath, just below the castle where we now stood, and well covered by the castle guns. The Royalists didn't really want to fight at all.

As you may guess from this unusual attitude, Rupert was not present. He was on his way, but not due for a good few days. Charles's fervent hope was that Parliament delayed hostilities until Rupert and his cavalry arrived.

But 17,500 Parliamentarians had other ideas. Under the Earl of Manchester, and boasting Oliver Cromwell's cavalry, they came to Newbury in a massively aggressive frame of mind and with the solid intention of attacking the Royalists wherever they could find them.

Probably most aggressive was the infantry's Sergeant Phillip Skippon. He had that kind of pent-up, frustrated anger that comes from fighting alongside Essex for too long. Essex had learned nothing from his one and only success at Newbury One, and had headed off to Cornwall, much against the wishes of most of his contemporaries. While there, he finally managed, bit by bit, to get his army comprehensively destroyed. The dazed remnants of his campaign staggered from the West Country to join Manchester's men. And they'd been forced to leave in the most humiliating way – leaving behind all of their guns and equipment, while Essex got a boat home. Skippon was one of those stragglers, and so very eager to avenge a hugely unpleasant year.

Having assessed Charles's troop deployments, Manchester and co. decided that a full, head-on frontal attack against such well-dug-in defensive positions would be suicidal. So they developed a rather clever tactical plan unlike anything the war had seen so far. Abandoning the usual massed-troops routine, the Parliamentarian army split in two, with a large section under Sir William Waller embarking on a fifteen-mile overnight march around the outskirts of the battlefield.

On the morning of 27 October 1644, Waller's men overran a Royalist outpost. With this short and decisive action, Parliament held both ends of the battlefield. The Royalists were stuck in the middle. Which wasn't a great place to be.

Parliament's plan was to attack simultaneously from both directions, sandwiching the Royalists in the centre . . . and slaughtering them, basically.

Whether William Waller had any idea what the word 'simultaneous' actually meant is unrecorded. But when Manchester attacked that morning, Waller did not. The result was exactly what Parliament had been trying to avoid in the first place – a full-on attack against heavily fortified positions from one direction only. The only difference was that Manchester had only half the manpower to do it with.

The outcome was rather predictable. Manchester sustained awful casualties and was driven back. To make matters even worse, as his men retreated they were pounded with artillery.

But it wasn't over yet by a long way. Which couldn't be said for my stay at the castle.

Dave was a mistake. Not in birth terms, as far as I know, but it was certainly a mistake bringing him along. He'd professed an interest in the Civil War and a strong desire to accompany us. At least I think that's what he said. I heard Civil War in there somewhere, but with hindsight I now think I may have corrupted 'I'd like to visit the battlefield with you' from 'I'd like to get very, very drunk and call you a twat all day long'.

Either way, I was now outnumbered by pub fans. They'd seen a pub at the bottom of the hill and couldn't get it off their minds.

'Good view of the battlefield isn't it, mate,' huffed Pete, finally drawing alongside me.

'It is, well . . . one part of the battlefield anyway, and this castle is incredible. You see all these mounds around it in a sort of star shape? They were dug by the Royalists as extra defences. And see those huge holes in the castle wall, they came from Parliamentarian cannonballs. And just over there . . . '

'Yeah, yeah, whatever,' said Pete, turning on his heels and starting back down the hill. 'Are we going to this pub or not?'

'Hang on, I need to make some notes.'

'Jusmakem danpub ye'twat,' explained Dave.

'What?'

'Yerchuffin nuts. Dooyer chuffin nuts danpub. So . . . thoucumming or arntcha?'

Whatever he'd said, we all headed down the hill. I decided I'd do my notes in the pub.

The Three Horseshoes was OK. The Ushers beer was OK. The décor was very football-orientated but OK.

The Newcastle United paraphernalia dotted around the room was a few hundred miles removed from where it should be, but OK.

But it wasn't OK that the pub lay a few hundred yards from the castle, and yet didn't acknowledge it, or the local battle, in any way whatsoever. Not OK with me, anyway. Pete and Dave happily reached a running total of four pints by half-past twelve, so all was well with their world. A quick bar chat with a couple of locals, in full earshot of the bar staff, revealed that nobody in the pub knew there had ever been a battle in this area. The castle was besieged, they said (which it was, for almost two years) but they didn't know anything about any big battles.

Again I was left with the distinct impression that the Civil War has been almost expunged from popular history. If it weren't for organisations like the Sealed Knot in this country, I'd have felt quite alone in my anorak-hood. Everybody knows how many wives Henry VIII had, and how Elizabeth I liked beheading her friends, but the Civil War is so neglected that people who actually live on seventeenth-century battlefields have no idea that they do.

Very sad. As was the conversation going on between my companions at the bar who, in fact, I now regarded more as luggage than companions.

'Avwetoo goater morfriggin castlesthen, or what?'

'Goats? Up at the castle? Didn't see any.'

'Nah yanumpty, whatyaonbout goats for? Sednuthin boutagoat?'

'Well, it's certainly the terrain for them, mate.'

With that they both returned to their pints and stared at the optics.

A person standing behind me suddenly tapped me on the shoulder, causing me to very nearly choke on Coke, nodded in Dave's direction, and whispered in my ear, 'Where's yowa mate from like, ah canna understand a word he's saying there, man?'

'Are you a Geordie?' I responded, realising I was very probably addressing the pub landlord.

'Aye.'

'He's from Leeds. You're from further north than he is. Can you really not understand him?'

'No man. By, I've heard some accents in my time, burra never heard owt like that, like.'

We nodded solemnly. Dave was untranslatable – even in the North. There was no hope for a Southerner. This gave me a massive sense of relief.

My next stop was Shaw House – the battle's other Royalist stronghold. Shaw House is famous for a certain brass plaque within its stately walls, and I couldn't wait to see it. But things were not going well that day. Shaw House was closed. Scaffolding adorned its entire bulk, and the constant sound of hammering, strangely reminiscent of musket fire, echoed from within.

I was refused entry by three men in hard hats, and so had to content myself with reading an information board outside the gates. Happily, it showed a close-up photo of the shield-shaped plaque:

The hole in the Wainscot which appears thro
the aperture of this plate was occasioned by a

> ball discharged from the musket of a
> Parliamentary Soldier at King Charles I while
> he sat dressing himself in this Projection. The
> ball was found and preserved during many
> years but is now lost. This Regicidal attempt
> seems to have been made on October 26th or
> 27 AD: 1644

What an incredible thing it would have been if the shot had hit and killed Charles. That Parliamentarian soldier came within a whisker of changing our whole national history. Would it have brought the war to an end at that moment? Possibly, but I definitely think that it would have ended the war in 1644.

With Charles dead, would the country have then opted for a Republic? I don't think so. I think that Charles's successor to the throne, the future Charles II, would have succeeded his father there and then. I also think that agreement between the new King, his advisors, and Parliament could have been reached, although Queen Henrietta Maria may well have had something to say about it.

But if agreement *could* have been reached, consider how that would have changed our history. The whole of the non-monarchy period from 1646 to 1660 wouldn't have happened. Oliver Cromwell would probably be only a marginal historical figure, never having been more than a Civil War general. Never would he have carried out the unification and reforms that shaped our nation, and never would he have had the chance to cause the hatred in Ireland, after his brutal invasion and conquest, that has tainted feelings to this day.

But, with no alternative history cutting in to change my present-day reality, Shaw House remained out of bounds, and we had no choice but to carry on to the village of Shaw's only pub, the Cock Inn. Pete was delighted. I think Dave was delighted too, but I'm not at all sure. I certainly caught a 'WAHEY' in there somewhere.

Now it was their turn for a shock. The Cock Inn was covered in scaffolding too. Its interior was totally gutted, as were they. It was time to move on. Shaw was closed for renovation.

In truth, I was struggling with where exactly to carry on *to*. This was probably the most confusing battlefield I'd visited. There were absolutely no markers, signs or information boards, and what gave it the edge on Newbury One was that this battlefield was probably just about everywhere, but nobody knew for sure which bits were where, and which bits weren't battlefield at all. Also, local awareness was totally absent. I asked around twenty people during the course of the day, and not one had any idea about the battle, or where any part of the battlefield might remain.

My only certainty was that a good deal of fighting had taken part on Speen Heath. As my earlier enquiries had revealed that most of Speen Heath is now a golf club, it had to be the nineteenth hole at Donnington Grove Hotel and Country Club for us!

A few minutes later we were cruising down lanes surrounded by beautifully manicured greens and fairways. I pulled up at the club's huge stately country house, and told the two semi-drunks in my car to wait five minutes while I asked for information in reception.

Stepping into the hotel foyer, I was immediately hit by a feeling of inadequacy. There is something about these places that does it to me. I glanced around at the beautiful decor and at the waistcoated staff, and that old sense of being a scruffy little oik in an upper-class establishment hit me full-on.

I don't know why this happens. I feel like a schoolkid, totally out of my depth. I've eaten at places like this a few times, but I always feel socially inferior to the waiters. This is a strange reaction, I know, especially in situations where I'm the paying diner, and they are waiting on me.

I walked sheepishly to the main desk, and felt totally ridiculous asking the receptionist whether she had any details about the battlefield her golf course was built on. The response was rather perplexing.

'How many, sir?'

'Pardon?'

'How many was it, sir?'

How many was it? How many fought in the battle? How many battlefields (and was this a philosophical question perhaps)? How many golf courses? I went for soldiers, merely because it was the only one I could answer with certainty.

'Well, about 20,000 men.'

The receptionist looked up at me for the first time, and frowned deeply.

'You want lunch for 20,000?'

'Eh, no, I didn't ask for lunch, I asked you if you had any information on the battle?'

'The battle? I think you'll need to speak to the manager.'

With that, she picked up a phone, tapped in some numbers and waited.

I waited too. We waited in total silence for what seemed an extraordinarily long time.

Eventually, she made contact: 'A gentleman in reception would like to know about battles? No . . . I don't know . . . that's all he said . . . OK thanks, I'll tell him.'

She replaced the handset and, fixing me with the most patronisingly huge smile I have ever seen, said, 'I'm sorry, sir. We don't have anything like that here.'

With that the matter was clearly closed. She returned to her notes and didn't look up again.

I wandered outside to the picturesque patio and lawn, strewn with tables and drinkers either smartly dressed or in golfing attire. One particular table was rather noisy. Among this merrymaking group of golfers and businessmen were two rather scruffy-looking men who should have been waiting in a car. They were swilling back beer, laughing heartily and . . . Pete appeared to be holding a handgun.

This was unexpected. He does an awful lot of stupid things, but he hadn't yet shot anybody.

As I watched, trying to make sense of a scene that couldn't possibly be happening, Pete raised the gun to his own head and pulled the trigger. Nothing happened. For a split second nothing happened. Suddenly, Pete's head slumped forward onto the table.

I stared aghast. How on earth could this have happened? How, in the space of around ten minutes, had Pete gone from sitting in my car, happily listening to nonsensical chat from his co-passenger, to shooting himself in the head in full view of a huge throng of lunchtime golfers?

This was unusual, even by his standards.

A great cheer went up from the table. Pete's back received a number of slaps, and then he was upright again, passing the revolver to an Oriental-looking gentleman in patterned yellow tank top, green shirt and plus fours, who immediately pressed it to the side of his head. It was like watching an upmarket golfing version of *The Deer Hunter*.

He pulled the trigger. There was a loud bang. I jumped out of my skin. The Oriental gentleman rocked in his chair for a moment, and then slapped the pistol down on to the table and groaned loudly. A round of applause went up.

I walked briskly to the table.

'Chris! All right, mate?' bellowed Pete. 'Just starting a new round. Are you in?'

'Round of what? What are you doing?'

'Russian Roulette, with a cap-gun revolver! It's brilliant. These guys play it all the time! You get a little reel of ten caps, you take out nine, spin the barrel and play. It's just like the real thing . . . except you don't die.'

I had to admit it was an extremely inventive use of a cap-gun, and an excellent gambling game. A little disconcerting for the uninformed onlooker though.

While Pete, Dave and co. pretended to blow

their brains out for a pound a try, I asked in the bar about the battlefield. Nobody had a clue. All I could do was guess.

And by my estimations, I was standing on the battlefield. I had to be. I was on Speen Heath, and just above us loomed Donnington Castle, so Royalist guns must have pounded this area. But nowhere was there any memorial or marker.

Fitting maybe, though, that the most confused battle of the entire war should have been fought on a battlefield that is now itself confusing.

And it certainly was a confused battle. The mix-up over attack times that caused Manchester to come to grief in the morning caused Waller the same problems in the afternoon. Waller finally attacked at 3 p.m. Another headlong assault from one direction only, with half an army.

Surprisingly, though, his attack caused problems. The sudden Royalist realisation that their enemy was coming from behind, and that their position was effectively surrounded, caused initial panic in the lines. Waller took full advantage, driving the Royalists back towards the village of Speen. For a few moments, it looked as if the Royalists would break.

But they didn't break. Once panic had subsided and discipline returned, superior Royalist numbers told. Waller had too few troops to hold his new positions. His advance ground to a halt, a gradual Parliamentarian retreat became rapid, and then a massed Royalist counter-attack swept Waller's men back with substantial casualties.

Around an hour later, Manchester attacked again,

but again the small size of his force and the continued lack of co-ordination in Parliament's attacks made his task hopeless. Only Cromwell came close to success, and what a story he almost created. A sudden surprise cavalry attack on the Royalist left-flank positions on Speen Heath came when a certain King Charles, and also his son the Prince of Wales, were visiting their troops. The two immediately fled the scene, but Cromwell had seen them go and rallied his men to pursue. In an effort to prevent their King's capture, his Life Guard Troops galloped out to meet Cromwell's Ironsides head on – never a good idea. They were cut to ribbons, but their brave delaying action allowed Charles and son to reach safety beneath Donnington's guns.

Another near miss. Charles was certainly sailing close to the wind that day.

After that high-octane incident, even Cromwell could make no further impression on the well-defended Royalist positions. In all, the day was a confused mishmash of botched Parliament attacks that ultimately led nowhere. The only truly happy Parliamentarian at Newbury was Sergeant Skippon, who managed, during the course of the battle, to recapture six of the cannon he'd walked away from in Cornwall!

As darkness fell, and the fighting petered out, it was the Royalists, interestingly, who thought they'd lost the battle. This was odd. The heavily fortified Shaw House had resisted all attempts of an attack all day, its well-placed musketeers and artillery inflicting heavy losses on any approaching bodies of Parliamentarians. Donnington Castle was under no threat at all, and the

Royalist field army had inflicted terrible casualties on the opposition without losing an inch of ground.

It was an excellent piece of defensive warfare. But Charles wasn't happy. From his point of view, the overall Royalist position was decidedly risky. Whether they'd held out unfalteringly or not, his army were still in the middle of fields, surrounded by Parliamentarian forces. His one thought was to get out. By moonlight, the Royalists withdrew from the battlefield and headed for Oxford.

In the morning, a peeved Cromwell and Waller, annoyed at the absence of an enemy, made loud noises about following them. But Manchester looked at his bloodied army and decided against a pursuit. It was probably a poor decision. The Royalists had moved from their entrenched positions, were an inferior force out in the open, and were now without the security of Donnington's artillery back-up. A pursuit would have been Parliament's best chance.

Pursuing any signs of that battlefield, we carried on around its long boundaries, searching for clues.

It was impossible. No markers, no signs, no monuments. Another total failure by local authorities to celebrate, or even mark, their own history. But while knowing which local authority to blame in each case, the real question was: 'Which local authority . . . and when?' There had been hundreds of years of local authorities between the Civil War and now. Which one should I blame – the 1750s' committee perhaps? Or the 1870s' council? The current incumbents were the only people I had to write to, but I knew I'd only get some budget report citing reasons why a monument and signs might possibly have to wait another couple of centuries. I felt my blood pressure rising yet again. The milkman was in for another bad morning's reading.

Under severe mental pressure from my passengers, I pulled into yet another pub – insisting it should be the last. We'd completed about eight full circuits by now, and were back near Donnington Castle yet again. The pub, fittingly, was named the Castle at Donnington.

We'd saved the best pub until last, it would seem. And within its walls, I was about to endure one of the most bizarre conversations of my life.

It all started well enough. The pub was excellent, a little modernly decorated for my taste, but tastefully so; hops dangling from its ceilings and walls, an art theme of old-style French theatre promos and café life, and a smart little walled courtyard garden. The beer on offer was perfect too – my beloved Timothy Taylor Landlord available in the one pub I was having a pint in! With Flowers Original and Fuller's London Pride also on tap (interesting bit of trivia – the current Fuller's site first started brewing during the Civil War), we were all happy, but as Dave got more and more plastered, you wouldn't have thought so.

'I've got eight legs,' said Dave.

Good. Heard that one clear as a bell. A quick count, however, proved that he was dramatically overestimating.

I smiled at him politely and sipped my drink.

'My chimney is the tallest and grandest in all Yorkshire,' continued Dave.

I smiled again, and stared into my beer.

'I've never had a banana though,' he said, shaking his head.

This time he was staring at me. He clearly expected some kind of response. I glanced at Pete.

Pete shrugged helplessly.

'Eh, a banana?' I said.

'Ye what?'

'No bananas? Ever?' I said, trying to sound sympathetic.

'Why ye on bout 'nanas, ye twat?'

Nope. He'd obviously said nowt about fruit. And very likely nothing about grand chimneys or surplus limbs. I was going to have to come clean.

'Look, Dave, I'm really sorry, mate, but I've got to admit that I haven't got the faintest idea what you just said. In fact . . . to tell the truth, I've never understood anything you've ever said to me.'

An initial look of hurt surprise was quickly followed by a frown, and then by a look of happy realisation, as if a deeply troubling conundrum had suddenly become clear.

'Ah . . . ' he said, grinning broadly.

'Ah,' I replied, grinning back.

'Our lass won't dance with us,' he said suddenly, thumping the table violently.

'What? Won't she, eh, sorry to hear that, why won't she?'

He frowned deeply. This was beginning to look like trouble.

'YOU WON'T, NOT "SHE" . . . YOU WON'T DANCE WITH US!!!'

He was right on that score.

'Eh, Dave, I know I must have this wrong, but I'm getting this as you're upset because I won't dance with you?'

'DANCE WITH US, YE TWAT, NOT DANCE WITH US, FOR FUCK'S SAKES!'

Pete got it. Belatedly he'd worked it all out: 'He wants you to dance with him, Chris.'

'But, but, there's not even any music . . . what am I saying . . . I'm not dancing with any bloke anyway. No way.'

Dave stood up. I thought he was about to drag me to my feet and waltz me around the room. Pete supportively tucked his chair in so that Dave could reach me.

Instead, Dave grabbed my notebook and pen. After two or three minutes' frantic scribbling, he slammed the notebook down in front of me and departed to the gents, a clearly upset man.

> OK, I hope you can read better than you can hear.
>
> You said to me that you don't understand me . . . I said to you 'that's why you won't answer us'. Nothing about dancing at all. What the chuff is all the stuff about dancing. You twat.

Hmm. 'Answer us' . . . 'dance wi' us'. Similar I suppose. I breathed a deep sigh, mainly through an acute embarrassment that I'd failed to understand, even slightly understand, a mere regional accent (which nowadays is extremely politically incorrect, of course). But also through a sense of irrational disappointment that he didn't want to dance with me. It's been years since anyone has. Another body blow to my impoverished ego.

Dave returned to the table. There and then I made a strong commitment to myself to listen to every word this man said to me, to ask if not 100 per cent clear what was being said, and to answer him properly.

'I've pissed in an old man's chips halfway up Mount Kawasaki,' said Dave, with a tired sigh.

Perhaps not.

At 6 p.m. myself and two completely blathered companions left the pub, and found something odd. We all stopped short of the car and stared. On my bonnet was a long black wig. What the . . . ?

Who on earth would have taken the trouble to remove their wig in a quiet country lane, and lay it carefully on my bonnet?

'Is that a wig?' asked Pete.

'It is,' I confirmed.

'A scalped Cavalier, perhaps?' said Pete.

I placed the unusual gift on the pavement, and we headed home. If the owner of that wig should happen to read this book, I would be very grateful if you'd contact me. It's one of those odd little incidents that may never be explained I know, but if somebody could answer the question 'Under what possible circumstances did you feel it necessary to leave a long, black, top-quality wig on my car bonnet while I was in a pub in the middle of nowhere?' I will undoubtedly die a happier man.

Naseby

In which Pillock provides a monumental ending

The Battle of Naseby took place on 14 June 1645.

It was, without doubt, one of the most momentous, important and decisive battles ever fought on British soil.

The depleted, split, but still 9,000-strong Royalist army under Charles and Rupert were encamped around the Leicestershire town of Market Harborough, when the shock news reached them that the entire Parliamentarian army, headed by Thomas Fairfax and incorporating Oliver Cromwell's fearsome Ironsides, were only fifteen miles away and closing fast.

This was no accident. Gone were the days of Essex bumbling around the countryside until he accidentally bumped into thousands of Royalists and (Newbury aside) got beaten by them. This reorganised Parliamentarian army, the New Model Army, were strong, disciplined and deadly. They knew exactly where the Royalists were, exactly where they were going, and intended to make absolutely sure they never got there. As far as Cromwell and co. were concerned, the Royalist cause would die here, in the border lands of Leicestershire and Northamptonshire, in June 1645.

Within hours of the sobering information that 13,500 Parliamentarian troops were moving in for the kill came more bad news. A Royalist outpost at Naseby, Northants, had been completely overrun by the advancing enemy. Naseby lay only six miles to the south. It was too late for escape. Any Royalist flight would see them attacked and harried from the rear, and possibly overwhelmed before being able to mount any organised defence. Rupert and Charles held an emergency council of war. It was decided that battle formations should be established immediately. The Royalists would stand and fight.

Moving swiftly, Rupert occupied strong defensive positions on high ground facing Naseby across a sweep of open countryside. Across that sweep, Parliament's army assembled and watched the Royalists spread out along a one-mile front ahead of them, massed infantry at the centre, cavalry on the wings. Fairfax deployed his men in exactly the same manner . . . and then realised he'd made a slight error. He'd chosen absolutely perfect defensive ground. His army sat atop a high ridge with steep, rising fields all around. It was *too* good. Even Rupert wouldn't attack these positions. And Fairfax desperately wanted Rupert to attack him. This was a cunning leader, totally aware that a mass Parliamentarian charge across the open countryside ahead could be disastrous.

Know your enemy, goes the old saying. Fairfax

certainly knew Rupert, and he also knew that if he could make his army seem in any way vulnerable, if he could briefly flash Rupert a soft underbelly, then Rupert would be lulled into a false sense of optimism, and attack.

To the surprise of his men, therefore, Fairfax ordered them down from their excellent positions, and sent them forward to Naseby Ridge, still good elevated ground, but not nearly as good as where they'd been.

Rupert watched in astonishment. He saw the Parliamentarians on the move and, without even the slightest suspicion of a trick, sounded the attack.

First forward went Rupert and his cavalry. Parliamentarian dragoons, deploying in hedges along the side of the field, opened fire. The Battle of Naseby had begun.

Naseby was a battlefield I'd been really looking forward to. I'd read everything there was to read about that fateful day, and about the modern-day battlefield which had, according to reports, been treated respectfully and was still very clearly understood. After Newbury, this was good to hear.

I'd fully intended to spend two days at Naseby, and had provisionally booked overnight accommodation in Leicester. Amazingly, Pete was having none of it.

'I'm not spending a night in Leicester, no way, absolutely no way.'

'Why not? What's wrong with Leicester?'

'It's a rough old city, Leicester . . . well rough.'

'Rubbish, Lorraine comes from Leicester, it's OK.'

'She left the place pretty quick though, didn't she?

A night out in Leicester is NOT something I'm prepared to brave. I've got my boyish good looks to think about.'

'Look, don't be stupid, where have you heard all this rubbish?'

'A bloke in the pub. He delivers to a stationery shop in Leicester. He reckons it's so rough even their window envelopes get boarded up!'

With that, it was settled. We'd spend just the one day in Naseby, and if I wanted to go back, I'd be going on my own.

So, here we were, driving into the village of Naseby at the impressively early time of ten in the morning.

And I was about to *be* impressed, beyond my wildest dreams. The best had truly been saved until last. I was immediately struck by the signposts. Not by anything written on them as such, more the fact they were there. A Civil War battlefield with signposts! This was truly a first. An array of brown boards pointed in various directions – 'Battle Museum' said one, 'Battle Monument' said another. Amazing.

I decided that the museum would be a good place to start, so followed the sign to the outskirts of town. Another sign guided me on – 'Battle Museum ¼ mile'.

It was here that I encountered my first problem. I drove two miles out of town, and back again. Nothing. A few dotted houses, a farm, but no museum. I repeated the procedure three times, but to no avail. Eventually, I parked next to the ¼ mile sign and, leaving Pete whining in the car, got out and walked. If it was there, I'd find it on foot. It took me fifteen minutes. On a gate, hidden by foliage, hung the museum's sign. 'OPEN APRIL TO SEPTEMBER' it shouted. Good, then it would be open. I looked over the gate. Was this some kind of cruel joke? There was nothing there – just an empty field. Not even a derelict building. Just a field full of neatly trimmed grass.

I walked back to the car and fetched Pete. We stood looking at the field for a few minutes.

'What?' he said.

'No museum. There's a sign, but no museum . . . '

Pete thought this through for a moment. 'Good,' he said, and headed back to the car.

Walking back, I spotted a couple in their drive, and asked them about the mysterious lack of a museum. They were vaguely aware that they'd had a museum at some time or other, but had no idea what they'd done with it. I once had exactly the same problem with a pair of socks, so completely understood. They suggested I visit the monument. I did as instructed.

The view from the monument is breathtaking. It sits on Naseby Ridge, the location to which Fairfax moved his men in order to provoke the Royalist attack. Ahead still lies that sweep of open countryside stretching away to the village of East Farndon, and Rupert's original positions. The battlefield was here, still here, with some additional hedgerow, but still here, almost as it was in 1645!

The monument itself is around fifteen feet tall and very impressive. Even more impressive was the man standing beside the monument's knowledge of the battle. Dave Ringrose grew up in the Naseby area, and remembers playing on the battlefield as a child. I have to say that when Dave first introduced himself, my first concern was why everybody seemed to be called Dave, but as he talked, the battlefield took on a real magic for me.

He pointed out all of the various military positions in the fields, described how the battle started, with the Royalists charging forward from the ridge ahead, and how, as the Parliamentarian dragoons opened fire, the left-flank Roundhead cavalry under Henry Ireton rushed forward to meet the enemy.

My mind was floating. I knew the story well, but stood and listened in silence, imagining the huge battle that played out on these quiet, deserted fields. Ireton's cavalry had no chance. They were facing Rupert, and Rupert was as determined as ever, his troopers slamming into their foe with absolute fury. It was a rout.

Suddenly, Parliament's numerically superior force was in trouble. As their shattered left-wing cavalry fled the field, hotly pursued by Rupert, the entire Royalist line moved forward across the field.

Despite Fairfax's plan to provoke an attack, the sheer swiftness and determination of it were proving devastating. The Royalist infantry pushed steadily forward towards Parliament's infantry, whose proximity, just behind the ridge, meant that neither side could see one another. When Parliament's men finally marched to the top of the ridge, both sides were in for a shock. There was nothing but a matter of yards between them. The Royalists had no idea they had advanced so close to their enemy's front line, and Parliament had no idea the Royalists were upon them.

Both sides immediately opened fire, musket balls whizzing everywhere in a ridiculously close-quarters fire-fight. The fact that Parliament's troops were shooting downhill meant that most of their shots were high and flew way over Royalist heads, while the Royalist volley caused far more damage. There was no time to reload, there was no time to organise a pike-led formation. With a yell, both sides threw pikes to the ground, gripped muskets by their barrels and charged headlong at one another.

By this time, Cromwell's right-wing cavalry had engaged the Royalist left horse. With Cromwell busy, and the huge infantry fracas raging in the centre, it was down to Rupert's men to move in and assist their infantry. A stunning victory was suddenly and unexpectedly within Royalist reach.

But where was Rupert?

Rupert had left the field. He'd pulled exactly the same stunt he had way back during the war's first major battle at Edgehill – pursued a beaten enemy from the field, chased them all the way back to their own baggage wagons, and then gone on a looting spree. This time, his lack of discipline would prove catastrophic.

Meanwhile Cromwell's ruthless Ironsides polished off their opposing cavalrymen, and now, in Rupert's absence, they raced to the centre and unleashed a furious attack on the Royalist infantry. It was carnage.

While the Ironsides rained havoc from upon horseback, Parliament's infantry reorganised and surged forward. The Royalist lines disintegrated into a bloody, screaming mess. As they began to break and run, the slaughter increased, the Roundheads slashing them down at will. The King looked on from the rear in personal agony as his army fell and died.

At first, in anger, he tried to rally his desperately retreating soldiers, intending to throw in all his reserves and go for broke. An advisor urgently informed him that it would be far better to turn and flee as quickly as possible. After a moment's consideration, Charles left the slaughter-fields behind him and headed for safety.

On those fields, the Royalists continued falling. At Marston Moor, Newcastle's Whitecoats had refused to surrender and fought to the death. At Naseby it was the turn of a battle-hardened Royalist unit named the Bluecoats. They fought, and fought, and fought as wave after wave of Parliamentarian attacks diminished their numbers . . . until not one Bluecoat remained.

But still the killing wasn't over. Parliamentarians hunted down the running Royalists and butchered them wherever they stood. This time they were giving no quarter. The war had dragged on and now they were ending it. A total massacre took place in Naseby's surrounding villages and countryside.

I pulled into a church car park at a little village named Marston Trussell and strolled into the churchyard.

Something that strikes me when I come to these historical places of such high drama and terror is the tranquillity. Standing in the sunshine in this beautiful little churchyard, it was hard to imagine that many a fleeing Royalist had died in this very place. A large number of them famously ran into the enclosed space of the churchyard, and realised to their horror that they were trapped. Parliament's men closed in, and hacked and slashed away until all were dead. Now, the only sounds here were the whisper of breeze and the song of birds.

I looked into the hazy distance across the green fields stretching away from this idyllic spot, shrugged and walked back to the car, feeling a little down. I got into my seat and let out a deep sigh. It was then that I noticed the smell.

I looked at Pete in horror. The man had been responsible for some of the most unwholesome aromas I've ever had the misfortune to inhale, but this one was truly shocking. It was the smell of whisky. And Pete was holding one of the biggest hip flasks I'd ever seen. Its leather casing bore the embossed legend 'Pete's Hair of the Dog'.

The thing about Pete and whisky is that they don't mix. He may get drunk on copious amounts of beer on a regular basis, but he rarely touches the hard stuff. Because the hard stuff sends him doolally. And not just a little bit doolally – the full mental jackass. That riding the cow incident . . . whisky. A shameful deportation from the Isle of Wight . . . whisky. A police caution at London Zoo for trespass and harassing a penguin . . . the same.

'How much of that have you drunk?' I asked, fearing the worst.

'All of it!'

I studied my companion. His eyes were swimming and there was a huge, unnerving grin on his face. My initial instinct was to drive straight home, but I needed to visit the local pubs, and besides, what could Pete possibly do on a quiet Wednesday lunchtime? The answer to that question would come back to haunt me.

'Why are you drinking whisky on a midweek lunchtime anyway?'

'Celebrating!'

'Celebrating what?'

'This is it! Just today's pubs to go, and I'm two hundred quid up. I've won my bet!'

With that he punched the car roof so hard that I feared the ceiling would come crashing down around our ears. If cars had plastered ceilings, of course . . .

He was right, though. This was it – the end of the Mission. I felt a sudden elation. I'd done it! I'd seen something right the way through, instead of just talking about it. Sure I'd been pushed – well, forced – at the start, but once we were on a roll there was no way we were going to stop. A happy grin spread across my face, and without thinking I gave Pete a hefty slap on the shoulder. This was a mistake. He immediately assumed he was under attack, ducked sideways, feigned a left jab, and tried to grab my head. After a brief struggle and some appeasement, I started the car and we headed back to Naseby.

As I drove, my happy contentment continued to grow, despite the sudden wild interlude. I also realised with some surprise that I was actually happy for Pete that he'd won his bet, and then, with even greater surprise, it hit me that I'd actually grown to like this bloke as a friend, rather than an almost bearable drinking companion. Somehow, gradually and steadily over the course of the war, our arguing had progressed from bickering to knockabout, our insults from harsh and irritated to a bit of easily shrugged-off banter. From desperately suggesting he abandon the Mission at

Edgehill, here at Naseby I knew I was actually going to miss travelling the country with him. I was sorry it was all over.

Or was it over? There have been plenty of wars . . .

'Two hundred quid! I've won! Two hundred quid! Not a penny for you, dickwad – all mine, MWAHAHAHAHA!'

Then again . . .

We drove back into Naseby and, as we were passing my beloved monument again, I thought I'd have one last look.

BATTLE OF NASEBY
14 JUNE 1645
FROM NEAR THIS SITE
OLIVER CROMWELL
LED THE CAVALRY CHARGE
THAT DECIDED THE
ISSUE OF THE BATTLE
AND ULTIMATELY THAT OF
THE GREAT CIVIL WAR

. . . read the inscription.

I shuddered slightly. How incredible. How incredible that such a momentous event had happened right here, 360-odd years ago.

A few minutes later we were ordering drinks at the Fitzgerald Arms.

'SOD!' cried Pete at the barman.

Here we go, I thought.

'A pint of Sod, sir, certainly, anything else?'

'SOD!' cried Pete.

'Another pint of Sod, sir? Right you are. Will that be all?'

'NUTS!'

Pete was enjoying this. Banks and Taylor's oddly named beer (the mischievously abbreviated Shefford Old Dark) had afforded him the opportunity to shout obscenities at the bar staff, so all was well with his world.

I looked around the cosy, beamed lounge bar, complete with inglenook fireplace. Not only had I saved the best battlefield until last, I'd just stumbled upon one of the best battlefield pubs, on a par with the Boot and Shoe at Tockwith, and not far behind the Castle Inn. The entire room was covered in Civil War memorabilia. I was back in my Civil War Cuckoo Land. There were muskets, large battle maps and portraits of both Charles and Cromwell. It was perfect. A huge framed poster immediately caught my eye, featuring a posing pikeman and shouting, 'YOUR KING NEEDS YOU!' Excellent! I walked straight over to it. 'Join the Earl of Northampton's Regiment of Foote', it continued. The poster turned out to be a rather brilliant recruiting advertisement for the local branch of the Sealed Knot.

I rushed through to the public bar to see what more was on offer. For a moment I thought I'd changed centuries. The public bar was so violently different from the lounge that I was left quite disorientated for a second or two.

'Can I help you?' came a female voice from nowhere. I looked around me. I couldn't see anybody.

'I was just a bit . . . taken aback by this room,' I replied to the multicoloured void. Was I in an episode of *Doctor Who*?

The landlady's head suddenly shot up from below the bar, almost giving me a heart attack.

'Sorry,' she laughed, 'just putting some bottles away. It is a bit of a startling room, isn't it?'

It certainly was. Its main theme was bright purple, but there were so many splashes of loud colour here, there and everywhere that the overall effect was almost psychedelic. Even the pool table was an explosion – a vivid mixture of pinks, oranges, reds and yellows, with red and yellow balls losing themselves in the cloth. The place looked like an incredibly eccentric nightclub . . . right in the heart of a sleepy little Northants village.

The really amazing thing though, the truly stunning thing, was that I liked it. It was *so* bright, *so* gaudy, that it smacked of fun, pure out-and-out fun. I instantly envisaged an evening spent in an olde worlde bar, with a quick 10 p.m. flit through a magic door into another world. Perfect.

'If you're looking for the cat,' continued the landlady, 'it's out.'

I was about to speak, but stopped for a second. This seemed a rather bizarre thing for someone to say. Why on earth would I be looking for her cat? Did she think I'd come round to take it out for a meal or something?

'Your cat? No, what –'

'Your friend told me you like cats.'

Things became clearer.

'You write books about cats, he says. That's an interesting job.'

'I do, yeah,' I replied, relieved to get back to reality. 'Not at the moment though. I'm writing about the Civil War.'

'Well, you've certainly come to the right place,' she said, glancing out of the window and smiling.

'I know, best battlefield I've been to, and probably the best monument too. It must be about fifteen feet high!'

'Fifteen feet high? Oh, you've seen the *little* monument then . . . '

A few seconds later, I was babbling excitedly into a pint-guzzling Pete's ear. He'd had two Sods and now he was on a Tiger, and he wasn't listening, or indeed (judging by the state of his eyes) able to listen.

'I told them about *A Cat Called . . . A Cat Called . . .* ?? About Brum,' he slurred.

'I know, Pete, listen, there's another monument, even bigger, just down the road, I'll nip down to it and pick you up in half an hour, OK?'

'Oh no you don't,' he rasped into my face. 'If my buddy Chris wants to see a monolith, then I'm your man. Just tell me where to go.'

'You what?'

'Lead the way,' he said, polishing off his pint. 'Let's go see what all this noise is about.'

Reluctantly, I took him with me. I saw the monument before I reached it. It was poking up above the trees! It was huge, absolutely huge, soaring over thirty feet into the sky! I bounded from the car (having remembered to stop it first) and straight across a bridged stream to the monument.

Its fading inscription wasn't the easiest to make out, mainly because it was about eight feet above my head, but having stared for a couple of minutes, the words came into focus:

TO COMMEMORATE
THAT GREAT AND DECISIVE
BATTLE FOUGHT IN THIS FIELD
ON THE XIV DAY OF JUNE MDCXLV
BETWEEN THE ROYALIST ARMY
COMMANDED BY HIS MAJESTY
KING CHARLES I AND THE
PARLIAMENT FORCES HEADED
BY THE GENERALS FAIRFAX
AND CROMWELL, WHICH
TERMINATED FATALLY FOR THE
ROYAL CAUSE, LED TO THE
SUBVERSION OF THE THRONE,
THE ALTAR AND THE
CONSTITUTION, AND FOR YEARS
PLUNGED THIS NATION INTO THE
HORRORS OF ANARCHY AND CIVIL
WAR, LEAVING A USEFUL LESSON
TO BRITISH KINGS NEVER TO
EXCEED THE BOUNDS OF THEIR
JUST PREROGATIVE AND TO
BRITISH SUBJECTS NEVER TO
SWERVE FROM THE ALLEGIANCE
DUE TO THEIR LEGITIMATE

MONARCH. THIS PILLAR WAS
ERECTED BY JOHN AND MARY
FRANCES FITZGERALD, LORD AND
LADY OF THE MANOR OF NASEBY.
MDCCCXXIII

I was unbelievably impressed. I found myself repeating the words over and over. My milkman could rest easy – Naseby ticked every box.

'Marvellous, isn't it?' said a man who'd just stepped up beside me.

'It is!' I enthused. 'How high do you reckon it is?'

'I'd say around thirty to forty feet. My name's Patrick, by the way. I heard in the pub that you're a writer?'

News travels fast in Naseby.

'Yeah, I am. I'm writing about the Civil War,' I replied. 'I've been travelling around all the battlefields, and half of them haven't even got a proper monument at all. Makes me sick to be honest . . . but this! This is fantastic!'

We turned as one and looked out in silence across the fields. Naseby has a real atmosphere about it, and it was exhilarating just to stand and take it all in. My mind drifted again, until I felt that I could almost hear the thunder of cannon and horses, could see the great clouds of gun smoke drifting across those meadows.

We stood for quite some time. My new companion finally broke our reverie, turning back towards the monument with a deep sigh.

'Is that idiot with you?' he said suddenly, an element of alarm in his voice.

I really didn't want to turn around. I really, really didn't want to know what terrible thing that whisky-fuelled maniac had done, or was doing, that could cause a total stranger to describe him as an idiot.

I slowly, very slowly, looked over my shoulder. Pete was nowhere to be seen. I looked at Patrick, and felt a shudder of panic course through me when I realised he was looking *up*.

I followed his gaze. About ten feet up the monument hung Pete. Worse still was his lack of trousers. I stared in sheer speechless bewilderment.

'No, he's not with me,' I said, noticing for the first time that Pete's corduroy trousers were ripped to shreds and hanging on the monument's iron-spiked protective fence. At that moment I remembered Pete's loyalty to me at the Battle of Marston Moor . . . well, in a pub in York, at least. I changed my plea.

'Er, he is with me actually, but I'm not sure why he's doing that. I'll sort it out.'

Patrick looked at me, looked up at Pete whose arms and pasty-white, hairy legs were wrapped tightly around the obelisk's slim girth, and burst out laughing.

'I'll leave it to you then, my friend,' he chortled and did exactly as he threatened, leaving me alone beside the monument, and ten feet below a drunken psychopath.

'PETE, GET DOWN, YOU PILLOCK!' I hollered.

'Pardon?' he called back.

'I said get down, GET DOWN!'

'They're fine,' called back Pete. 'I'll keep my eye on them.'

'Who?'

'I'm climbing this monument.'

'I know, get down here now.'

Pete began climbing upwards. As he went up, his underpants crept disconcertingly downwards. By the time he'd covered another two feet, he was presenting a full moon. It was horrific.

An elderly lady, passing by on the other side of the bridge, stopped and stared. I'm not sure if she was really able to take it all in, because after a few moments of staring at an obese half-naked giant shuffling up a forty-foot monument, she simply carried on her way as if this was a fairly normal thing for Wednesdays.

I slumped on the grass and watched helplessly. Suddenly, he began climbing down. Halfway to the bottom he stopped and, clinging on with one arm like a giant baboon, managed to haul up his briefs, mumbling something about terrible chafing.

He reached the fence, climbed recklessly to its top, nicked his leg on a spike and belly-flopped eight feet onto the grass. I rushed to his aid. He didn't move at first. And then, lying face down on the ground, he began twitching and groaning. Finally he turned his head to me and coughed.

'I'm a goner; you go on without me,' he rasped.

'Go where? Are you OK?'

'I knew I wouldn't make it to the end of this war, mate. So close, so close . . . '

'Cut the dramatics, Pete –'

'Go, go,' he cried, flinching in pain. 'Save yourself.'

I stared at the stricken Pillock. There was a little truth in his drunken ramblings. How fitting that he'd survived through all our travels thus far, only to fall here at Naseby, like the Royalist cause before him. The only difference was that the Royalist demise smacked of romance and heroism. This trouserless drunken lump gasping for breath on the grass brought to mind neither.

'Get up, you lunatic,' I said.

'OK, just give me a minute.'

After half an hour he finally let me tip him into the car, and we headed for home.

My journey through Civil War England was over, and so too was the Great Civil War itself. Over bar the shouting, at least. What was left of the Royalist army carried on bravely after their terrible ordeal at Naseby, but it was a token struggle. The King's stronghold of Oxford was surrendered to Parliamentarian forces in 1646. Charles was tried, and eventually beheaded in 1649. General civil unrest, war, riot and rebellion would be a constant part of British life for the next two decades. But not all was bleak – there was still bubonic plague and the Fire of London to look forward to.

At the end of it all, the British monarchy was restored by popular consent, Charles II was crowned King of England in 1660, and things returned to pretty much the way they were before it all started . . . but for one major difference.

Never again would a British monarch dare to claim absolute power. Control would continue to drift inexorably in the direction of Parliament. By the time the next Charles comes to the throne, in fact, he will have little to do but moan about buildings and talk to vegetation . . . which he actually does rather well.

But if he dares to suddenly claim divinity (which I suppose isn't beyond the realms of possibility), dismisses Parliament and invades Scotland, he's going to have problems.

I for one will be donning helmet and breastplate, dusting down a pike and marching out to meet him on some great sweep of open countryside. And, while the beer is still in Parliament's possession at least, I'm sure that a fat slob in an ill-fitting uniform will be marching by my side, pike under one huge arm, toilet seat under the other. Ready to take on the world.

Where Are They Now?

What became of the gallant heroes of the First Civil War? And what became of Essex?

King Charles I

Charles was charged with 'High Treason Against the People of England', and tried in January 1649. Predictably, he refused to answer the charges or accept the authority of the court.

He was subsequently beheaded at Whitehall on 30 January 1649, and buried at Windsor. His death caused outrage and shock throughout Europe.

To this day, on 30 January every year, wreaths are laid at his statue, which stares down Whitehall to the place of his execution.

Prince Rupert

After the Great Civil War, Rupert was exiled by Parliament, and so became involved in a little fighting in France. He soon got back to harassing Parliament, returning in a Royalist naval role and attacking by sea during that not-so-great and ill-fated uprising, the Second Civil War.

Ever colourful, he then became a buccaneer, attacking English shipping off the West Indies!

After the Restoration of the Monarchy in England, and the crowning of Charles II, Rupert returned to England and was soon fighting the Dutch for us.

He finally hung up his boxing gloves in 1674 and became a scientist, accredited with the invention of a printing process, a type of gunpowder and – most interestingly of all – Rupert's Balls. Rupert's Balls are small glass bulbs, created by dipping molten glass in cold water. While the bulbous end of the bulb is strong enough to withstand a strike from a hammer, the small end explodes with ferocity at the slightest touch. Rupert used these things as a joke, demonstrating their toughness, and then handing them to unsuspecting courtiers . . . who almost blew their own hands off.

So, heartwarmingly, it would appear that Rupert never lost his almost childlike urge to cause pain and bloodshed wherever possible, even as an ageing dignitary in Royal Court.

Somewhat surprisingly, for a man who spent virtually his whole life at war, Rupert died quietly at home on 19 November 1682.

The Earl of Newcastle

After the destruction of his Whitecoats at Marston Moor, Newcastle exiled himself to the Continent.

But, following the Restoration in 1660, he returned to England and was made a Knight of the Garter in 1661, and a Duke in 1665.

He never received, however, the place in high office that he felt his loyalty and huge personal expenditure during the Civil War merited. A little sulkily, he moved away from public life and spent his last years writing and breeding horses.

He died on Christmas Day 1676, and is buried at Westminster Abbey.

The Earl of Essex

Essex's disastrous campaign in the West Country proved to be his last, and he resigned his commission a few months later, giving a memorable and dignified speech in the Commons.

The following year, he went out hunting stags, and lost.

He received a huge funeral, and was buried in Westminster Abbey in September 1646 – the official cause of death, a massive stroke.

Sir Thomas Fairfax

Fairfax continued as Lord-General of the Army after the Civil War, and played a full part in crushing the rebellions of the Second Civil War.

After many years of fighting and political intrigue, he finally retired from public life following the Restoration, and lived quietly until his death in 1671.

Fairfax is buried at Bilborough parish church near York.

Oliver Cromwell

Cromwell fought on during the years of insurgency and war following the First Civil War, defeating in turn the Irish, Scots and all Royalist attempts to regain power.

He finally claimed power in England in the most ironic way. Considering that the whole rebellion had started with Charles bursting into the Commons with an armed escort and dissolving Parliament, you'd have thought that Cromwell might have avoided bursting into Parliament with a band of musketeers and doing exactly the same thing. But that's what he did. He'd grown impatient with Parliament's inability to come to agreement over . . . well, anything really, and so replaced them with a 'Nominated Assembly' of his own choosing.

Six months down the line, the Nominated Assembly were deemed to be doing little better than their predecessors, and power was handed to Cromwell.

Cromwell became 'Lord Protector' in 1653 and, in a final twist of the knife, moved into Charles's former palace at Whitehall. By 1656 he was being referred to as 'Your Highness' and handing out knighthoods. In 1657, a group of MPs even offered him the Crown, which, to his credit, he refused. He was, however, regarded by the country as 'king in all but name'.

He died of malaria on 3 September 1658, having nominated his son to succeed him. Within a year, his Protectorate was abolished.

Cromwell was buried at Westminster Abbey, but in 1661, obviously without a hint of bitterness over the Civil War and the execution of his father, Charles II ordered his body to be exhumed, hanged and decapitated.

His head remained on a pole for another quarter of a century, and is now buried in the chapel of Sidney Sussex College, Cambridge.

Peter Ilic

Pete recovered from the horrific injuries sustained at Naseby, but never quite recovered from the disappointment of unexpectedly losing his £200 bet. A disagreement on exactly what constitutes a major battlefield, and a lack of forethought in specifying the word 'major' in the first place, meant that Pete was judged to have fallen a few thousand pubs short of his target. His creditors have yet to receive a penny.

Pete has now become a memorial statue to himself. The statue can be found propping up the public bar of the Prince of Wales, Great Kingshill, Bucks, every week-night and all day Saturdays.

Appendix

The Battle of Edgehill, 23 October 1642
Royalist army: just under 15,000; Parliamentarian army: just over 15,000
OS Landranger map: 151; OS Explorer map: 206

The Carpenter's Arms, Banbury Street, Kineton, CV35 0JS Tel: 01926 640364

The Castle Inn, Edgehill, Nr Banbury, OX15 6DJ, Tel: 01295 670255

The Swan Hotel, Banbury Street, Kineton, CV35 0JS, Tel: 01926 640876

The Rye, December 1642
Royalist army: 5,000; Parliamentarian army: circa 4,500
OS Landranger map: 175; OS Explorer map: 172

The Pheasant, 99 London Road, High Wycombe, Buckinghamshire, HP11 1BU Tel: 01494 527138

The Pride/Office (now the Nags Head), 63 London Road, High Wycombe, HP11 1BN Tel: 01494 521544

The Battle of Chalgrove, 18 June 1643
Royalist army: circa 1,000 cavalry with infantry and dragoons at a distance but not engaged; Parliamentarian army: circa 1,150
OS Landranger map: 165; OS Explorer map: 171

The Crown, 96 High Street, Chalgrove, OX44 7SS
Tel: 01865 890273

The Lamb, 2 Mill Lane, Chalgrove, OX44 7SL
Tel: 01865 890295

The Red Lion, 115 High Street, Chalgrove, OX44 7SS
Tel: 01865 890625

The Battle of Adwalton Moor, 30 June 1643
Royalist army: circa 10,000; Parliamentarian army: circa 4,000
OS Landranger map: 104; OS Explorer map: 288

The Railway Inn, 1 Birstall Lane, Drighlington,West Yorks, BD11 1JJ Tel: 0113 287 9001

The First Battle of Newbury, 20 September 1643
Royalist army: circa 15,000; Parliamentarian army: circa 15,000
OS Landranger map: 174; OS Explorer map: 158

The Gun, 142 Andover Road, Newbury, RG14 6NE
Tel: 01635 47292

The Old Bell, 215 Andover Road, Newbury, Berkshire, RG14 6ND Tel: 01635 41510

The Battle of Marston Moor, 2 July 1644
Royalist army: 18,000; Parliamentarian army: 27,000
OS Landranger map: 105; OS Explorer map: 289/290

The Sun Inn, York Road, Long Marston, York, North
Yorkshire, YO26 7PG Tel: 01904 738258

The Boot and Shoe Inn, Marston Road, Tockwith, York, North
Yorkshire, YO26 7PR Tel: 01423 358232

The Spotted Ox, Westfield Road, Tockwith, North Yorkshire,
YO26 7PY Tel: 01423 358387

The Second Battle of Newbury, 27 October 1644
Royalist army: circa 9,000; Parliamentarian army: circa 17,500
OS Landranger map: 174; OS Explorer map: 158

Hare and Hounds Hotel, Bath Road, Speen, Newbury,
Berkshire, RG14 1QT Tel: 01635 521152

Donnington Grove Country Club, Grove Road, Newbury, RG14
2LA Tel: 01635 581000

The Castle at Donnington, Oxford Road, Newbury, Berks.
RG14 3AA Tel: 01635 40615

The Battle of Naseby, 14 June 1645
Royalist army: circa 9,000; Parliamentarian army: circa 13,500
OS Landranger map: 141; OS Explorer map: 223

The Fitzgerald Arms, Church Street, Naseby, NN6 6DA Tel:
01604 740273

All information was correct at time of publication.

Timeline

 The Battle of Edgehill,
October 23rd 1642

 The Rye,
December 7th (?) 1642

 The Battle of Chalgrove,
June 18th 1643

 The Battle of Adwalton Moor,
June 30th 1643

 The First Battle of Newbury,
September 20th 1643

 The Battle of Marston Moor,
July 2nd 1644

 The Second Battle of Newbury,
October 27th 1644

 The Battle of Naseby,
June 14th 1645

A t l
O c